MW00635650

Gypsy Magic

The Ultimate Guide to Romani Witchcraft,
Signs, Symbols, Talismans, Charms,
Amulets, Tarot, Spells, and More

Your Free Gift
(only available for a limited time)

Thanks for getting this book! If you want to learn more about various spirituality topics, then join Mari Silva's community and get a free guided meditation MP3 for awakening your third eye. This guided meditation mp3 is designed to open and strengthen ones third eye so you can experience a higher state of consciousness. Simply visit the link below the image to get started.

https://spiritualityspot.com/meditation

Table of Contents

Introduction

Gypsies are rightly famous for their psychic powers and unjustly and unfairly infamous for all the wrong things. This book is focused on the specific and wide-ranging magical and psychic abilities that have been passed down for generations of the Romani people. It does not deal with the unjust way the world treats the Romani people or those who do not or did not understand the power of magic and try to fit squares and rectangles into circles and spheres.

The gypsy world is filled with joy and happiness, despite gypsies' relentless struggles to fight for dignity and respect. The Romani people have stood by their own, fought against oppression and unfair discrimination, and come out strong, never letting go of their culture, even as they happily and humbly embraced the culture and religion of the places to which they moved and migrated.

This book gives you an in-depth study of the Romani people, their origins, and their migrations to different geographies. It discusses how they saved their culture, magic, and psychic powers. It gives you amazing insights into symbols and signs that the Romani could read and understand in ways non-Romani could never do.

This book deals with how the gypsies embraced the power of nature and used what Mother Earth gives in abundance to heal themselves and those in need. As they traveled around the world, the Romani picked up valuable lessons and tried to share them with others, even as they used them for their own good. They learned and embraced the connection between humanity and divinity and harnessed divine energy to improve their lives.

Read on to find a detailed, comprehensive guide on gypsy magic and how to use it to enhance the quality and meaning of your life. It is replete with all the information you need to learn and practice gypsy magic. So, go ahead and turn the page.

Chapter 1: Gypsy Witchcraft Basics

For centuries, gypsies have had a mysterious, exotic aura about them—or at least, that is how the non-gypsies view them. They have been nomads for generations, traveling around the globe and having no steady place they call home. Yet, they have an identity, a history, a name for themselves, and roots from ancient times.

For centuries, gypsies have had a mysterious, exotic aura about them.
https://www.pexels.com/photo/a-fortune-telling-session-in-progress-6944915/

There is an old saying among the Romani people that goes like this, "Ki shan i Romani/ Adoi san' i chov'hani," which translates to "Wherever gypsies go, there the witches are, we know." The Romani people, commonly known as gypsies, were nomads or eternal wanderers. Their magical practices and customs relied heavily upon an oral tradition. It is believed that they came to be known as "gypsies" in Europe because the Europeans thought they were from Egypt.

Understanding the Romani People

The Romani people (also referred to as the Roma) were as diverse as the geographies and populations of the world. They were also known by names aligned with their rooted culture. In Spain, they were called Gitanos. In France, they were named "gitan." In Central and Eastern Europe, they were called Tsingani. Across the Scandinavian regions, they were called by different words based on the local language, all of which translates to "traveler."

Interestingly, the Romani people called themselves by different names. In England and Portugal, the Romani called themselves Kale. In France, they called themselves Manush, and in western Europe and Germany, they called themselves Sinti. Regardless of where they lived, the Romani people were collectively called gypsies; a term used to refer to people who migrated all over the world over several centuries. Gypsies are those who never have a permanent home. Here are some intriguing and interesting facts about Romani people.

They originated in India. Based on linguistic analysis, experts believe that the Romani originated in the northern plains of India. Many of the words of the languages they speak are very similar to Hindi, one of the major languages spoken in India, especially in the northern parts of this Asian country.

Genetic evidence also suggests that the Romani have their roots in India. A 2012 study published in the *Journal of Cell Biology* involved collecting and analyzing people from numerous Romani cultures around the world. This study observed that the Romani people likely migrated from India about 1,500 years ago. Present-day European Romani people are believed to have traveled through the Balkans more than 900 years ago.

In India, they were called Doms, which translates to "men". Doms became Roms and then Romani right across Europe. However, in North

Africa and the Middle East, they call themselves Doms or Domi.

There are about twelve million Romani people globally. Experts opine that the Romani people left India about 1,500 years ago and mostly traveled to Europe. They are believed to have gone to some Eastern European countries such as Romania and Bulgaria. About twelve percent of the Romani people are found in these regions today. Turkey, Slovakia, Russia, Serbia, Hungary, France, and Spain also have a large Romani population.

While the Romani are found primarily in Europe, many have made other nations their home, too.

- About a million Romani have made the United States their home.

- There are about 800,000 in Brazil.

- Doms have also made many Middle East countries their homes, such as Iran, Cyprus, Lebanon, Syria, Israel, and Jordan.

Horrific discrimination and persecution have fallen upon the Romani people wherever they went. When they first migrated to the continent, the Europeans enslaved them.

Romani enslaved people were prevalent right up to the nineteenth century. Right through the Medieval Ages, the Romani people in Europe were persecuted, punished, and even sentenced to death for the flimsiest reasons, often without a simple trial. For example, in 1554, a law was passed in England that said the sentence for living like a gypsy was death.

Thanks to all the discrimination, persecution, and misplaced fear, the Romani people have been seen as thieving, cunning foreigners who steal and move on to the next place for more thieving. Yet, their power of magic was feared, too.

In Germany, gypsies were imprisoned indiscriminately and forced to do hard labor. After repeated attacks, many surviving gypsies formed violent gangs, initially hoping to protect themselves, but soon turned their violence against everyone.

In 1790, the King of Prussia saw the gypsies as an opportunity and converted it into an advantage both for his kingdom and for the gypsies. He decreed that all gypsy men should enlist in the military: A wise move that was followed by other European kingdoms. Since then, gypsy men have done military service for almost all European nations.

Countless reports of violent acts have been documented against them. For example:

- Romani children were abducted from their homes for slavery and prostitution.

- Women's ears were cut off.

- Hot irons were used to brand gypsies.

- Gypsies were prohibited from following their customs and rituals or speaking their language. Cultural and religious conversions were forced upon them.

- Intermarriage within the Romani community was forbidden.

The persecution of the Romani was at its worst during the Nazi regime. The BBC reported that they were the first targets of Nazi atrocities, followed closely by Jews and homosexuals. An estimated two million Romani are believed to have died in Nazi concentration camps. They were the guinea pigs for all evil Nazi torture and other extermination experiments.

Even today, they face discrimination and persecution and continue to fight for their rights. For example, some countries do not provide housing facilities to the Romani, even to those born in those nations. They end up living in metallic makeshift homes without access to water and sanitation. Some other countries do not hesitate to expel the Romani people.

However, in recent times, multiple Romani organizations have been formed to fight for their rights and stop discrimination and persecution. Further, many organizations have come forward to provide resources for the growth and development of the Romani people, especially through education.

The rich culture of the Romani people has been an inspiration for many musicians worldwide, most notably Franz Liszt, the famous classical composer. Gypsy music has inspired many genres of music, such as bolero, jazz, flamenco, etc.

Music played an important role in the life of the Romani people. The reason for this is quite obvious, considering that at the beginning of their migration from India, the Romani people's professions included music and dance, performances, etc.

Family was paramount among the Romani people. Families with similar dress codes, occupations, and language usually grouped together into "tribes." Each group had its own specific nationality, too.

Considering that they originated in India, the Romani were believed to be originally Hindus. However, they assimilated and adopted the religions of the various lands as they migrated and traveled across the globe. Today, most follow some form of Islam or Christianity, retaining a few of the original Romani customs and traditions.

The Romani People From Around the World

In India, gypsies were considered low-caste people who traveled around the country as singers and musicians. It is believed that in 430 BCE, an Indian king gifted 12,000 people from a low-caste tribe to Bahram V, a Persian King. These people made Persia their home for a while before moving to other parts of the Middle East and Europe. Some could have escaped from slavery, while others were kidnapped and captured by the Byzantines and then found their way into Syria and other Middle Eastern and European countries.

Gypsies traveled far and wide, much more than any other group of people. Their knowledge about the world and the happenings in the world was unparalleled. Therefore, rumors spread that they were used as spies, especially during wars.

European Roma

Most of the Roma in Germany and German-occupied territories in pre-war Europe belong to the Roma and Sinti tribes or family groups. They speak a Sanskrit-based dialect. Some follow Islam, while others are Christians.

In Europe, the term "Roma" includes both the Sinti and Roma tribes. Some of the Roma tribespeople prefer being referred to as "gypsies." Interestingly, in German, *Zigeuner*, which means "untouchable, is the word for gypsy.

The European Roma in pre-war Europe worked as artisans, performers, and craftsmen. They were blacksmiths, toolmakers, horse traders, tinsmiths, circus animal trainers, dancers, etc. There were a few Romani shopkeepers, too, in pre-war Germany. By the early twentieth century, the nomadic lifestyle was on the decline.

Before World War II, the population of Roma in Europe was over one million. Most of the gypsy population was concentrated in and around Eastern European countries, such as the former Soviet Union, Poland, Romania, etc. Western European countries, such as the former Yugoslavia, Bulgaria, Germany, and Hungary, also had a sizable Roma population. Many of the above Roma people faced horrific persecution during the Nazi regime, and their population declined considerably.

Egyptian Doms

As mentioned at the start of this chapter, the word gypsy was coined by Europeans when they mistook travel migrants from northern parts of India to have come from Egypt. However, there are gypsies from Egypt, too, most commonly called Doms, who are believed to have psychic and magical powers.

Today, gypsies found in Eastern Africa, including Egypt, Israel, Turkey, and Syria, are called Doms. Like the Roma in Europe, the Doms are marginalized and persecuted. Doms are not officially recognized in Egypt, thanks to a law connected with the country's national identity card. Only three religions are recognized in Egypt: Islam, Christianity, and Judaism. Anyone following any other religion or ethnicity is not issued a national identity card in Egypt. Therefore, Bedouins, Nubians, and, of course, Doms are not recognized in Egypt, and because of this, there is no official record of their population and related parameters.

The Doms of Egypt are divided into different tribes, including the Halebi, the Ghagar, and the Nawar. Sadly, these words are insults in Arabic. It is believed that Ghagar, which loosely translates to "vagrant," could be the largest Dom group. According to a 50-year-old ethnographic research survey conducted by the late Nabil Sobhi Hanna, the Ghagars lived outside villages, on the edges, as they were not allowed entry inside. They were donkey and horse dealers, entertainers, and ironsmiths.

More recently, they have migrated to Cairo. Unfortunately, most of them resort to begging when the income from dwindling trades is insufficient to meet their survival needs. Interestingly, although Doms now lead sedentary lifestyles, their professions continue to reflect their nomadic spirit. Most of the Doms occupy rented homes and move often. They take up short-term jobs and live on the edge of Egyptian societies.

Doms in the Middle East

In the Middle East, Doms lead a varied lifestyle. Some are still nomadic, lead peripatetic lives, and are entertainers, metal workers, musicians, and migrant workers. They work part-time in fields, especially during harvest seasons when you can see many Doms harvesting crops in the Jordan Valley. They also work in the tobacco fields of northern Jordan. A few Middle Eastern Doms are pastoralists. In Iraq, Doms still move around in their colorful caravans and wear costumes as dancers, fortune tellers, acrobats, jugglers, and musicians.

The Roma and Music

During the nineteenth century, gypsies were recognized for their excellent music skills, especially in Russia, Hungary, and Spain. Gypsy minstrels were an integral part of the Hungarian nobility. Dedicated minstrels played for guests during banquets, feasts, and other celebratory events hosted by Hungarian nobles. Nearly all Hungarian bands of royal families had at least one Romani violin virtuoso.

The Social and Family Life of the Romani People

As mentioned, the Romani hardly followed the social rules of an organized society. And yet, they had their own rules under an umbrella of a social and communal set of regulations called Romano, which governed things like hygiene and cleanliness within the homes, and in the community, respect for everyone, respect for justice, etc. Romano means to act and behave in a dignified manner with everyone.

According to the gypsy rules, they have arranged marriages wherein the groom's father approaches the bride's father to ask her hand in marriage for his son—the right to accept or refuse remains with the young couple. The groom's father had to pay a bride price, the amount of which depended on many factors, including the family's status, history, whether the bride had earning potential, etc.

After the marriage, the bride moves into her husband's house and lives with her in-laws. She is expected to do the household chores and look after her husband and his family's welfare. Many times, daughters are exchanged as brides. Thus, the daughter of one household becomes the daughter-in-law of another household, and the daughter of the second household becomes the daughter-in-law of the first.

The family is the most important unit among the Romani people, considering they have no country, kingdom, or republic to which they belong. Typically, a family consists of the head of the unit, his wife, their sons and daughters-in-law, unmarried adults, children, and grandchildren.

The Romani people also follow a social hierarchy beyond the family. About ten or more extended families—sometimes, the number of families could be as large as a hundred—grouped under a social and community umbrella are referred to as kumpania. Each kumpania travels in caravans as one big group. Within each band, small groups called vistas are formed and connected through common ancestry.

Here are some more interesting facts about the social structure of the Romani people:

- The head of a kumpania was called voivode. He held his position throughout his entire lifetime. The next voivode was elected when the previous one died.

- A post called "phuri dai" within every tribe existed. This post was usually held by a wise, old, and experienced Romani woman. She was in charge of looking after women's and children's issues in the kumpania.

- The display of wealth was considered a matter of pride among the Romani people and was considered honorable. They loved opulence. The women proudly wore ornate headdresses and gold jewelry. Gold and silver coins were used to decorate homes.

- Sharing and being generous with your wealth and resources was considered a matter of pride and honor, and food and drink were lavished on guests.

- Generosity and sharing were considered an ethical, moral investment they could call upon during bad times.

The Romani People, Religion, and Witchcraft

The Romani people do not have a single faith or religion they follow. More often than not, they embrace and adopt the religion of the host country. Therefore, in the Middle East, the Doms are devout Muslims. It is common to see Doms undertake the annual pilgrimage to Mecca.

There are Christian gypsies in many countries who follow various sects of Christianity, such as Anglican, Pentecostal, Baptist, and Catholicism. And yet, for the Doms, religion is very personal. They do not discuss or talk about their faith with people.

They are superstitious—they call it magic—and embrace the good elements of all religions. They are deeply spiritual, and spiritism is dominant in their way of thinking and understanding the world and how it works. They fear curses and evil spirits, and therefore, they are happy to help others ward off evil entities and curses through magic and witchcraft.

Even today, the Romani people fear the "mullo" or the ghost of a dead person. The fear of being haunted is so deep that they destroy everything that belonged to dead people, including their wagons, clothes, etc. By destroying all of these items, they believed that the ghosts of dead people would not have anything to return to and, therefore, would not come back to haunt the living people. In fact, the Roma of England even set fire to the wagon of the dead person.

The first adage mentioned in this chapter translates to "Wherever gypsies go, there the witches are, we know." For generations, the Romani people have made a living through fortune-telling. Interestingly, spices and their smells play a big role in witchcraft. Considering that it is believed that the Roma originated in India, it is no surprise that spices—also found extensively in India from ancient times—play such an important part in their lives and from their lives to their professions, one of which is witchcraft.

Gypsy women were known to be excellent spell casters and practitioners of witchcraft. Settled citizens of the countries they migrated to looked at gypsies with suspicion, considering they were wanderers with no permanent place they called home. Interestingly, not having a permanent place to call home did not dent their confidence and pride. Their primary focus is to live life on their terms. They dislike being bound by rigid societal rules that do not fit in with their culture and belief systems. Although they want the best for their children, they choose not to educate them in a bid to make them less "modern" and more attached to their own culture.

Interestingly, despite all the hardships they face, the gypsies cling to their magic and witchcraft, both of which are deeply integrated into their culture. While doubters and cynics around the world question the "power and sense" in doing magic, for the gypsies, the practice of magic is considered useful and productive. The magic they do and the graces and help they seek from the spirits can be equated with how non-gypsies pray to their gods, seeking some things such as the recovery of a lost love or item, protection against danger, a loving partner, etc.

Gypsies are divided into tribes, each with its own symbols and talismans. Most gypsies have basic powers such as spell casting, brewing potions, mediumship—the ability to connect and commune with the spirit world—and divination. There is nothing unique about magic and psychic powers. All of us are born with it. However, the Romani people are among the few who continue to believe in these inherent powers and work hard to cultivate their innate talents and improve their craft.

The gypsies had varying witchcraft beliefs depending on their geography and culture. For example, in some Romani cultures, horses were considered spiritual animals, and keeping a horse's skull was excellent for preventing evil paranormal spirits from entering your home. Most of the gypsy magic centered around nature, animals, plants, and the divine powers of these living beings.

Belief in the divine power of animals is why the Roma revered and valued their animals and cattle highly. They paid close attention to their animals, talked and interacted with them, listened to them, and tried to connect with their spiritual power. Animals were often part of magic rituals.

What non-gypsies call superstition is what gypsies believe are elements of magic and witchcraft. They use amulets, talismans, knots, and charms to enhance the power of their magical prowess. Magical symbols in gypsy magic include stones, knives, shells, and other natural elements. To reiterate, the Romani people tried to harness the magic from the power of nature.

The Roma Today

In the olden days, gypsies would walk through the streets, seeking hands to read and to foretell the future for those who wished to use their witchcraft services. Of course, payment in cash and/or in kind was the crux of the matter for the gypsies. Today, most of them rely on the Internet for their clients.

Also, today's nomadic Romani people use RVs and cars to move from place to place. Many Romani have also settled down and are not easily distinguishable from non-gypsies. In fact, thanks to the discriminatory attitude of society, some Romani people prefer to hide their roots.

And yet, there is a lot of effort to end discrimination and persecution against innocent Roma. Every year, April 8 is celebrated as the International Day of the Roma and is specifically used to spread awareness and celebrate the Roma culture worldwide.

Chapter 2: Lore, Codes, and Beliefs

The gypsy practices and beliefs are as diverse as the geographical nations in which they live. However, this chapter looks at the folktales and beliefs that are more or less common among all gypsies.

The gypsy practices and beliefs are as diverse as the geographical nations in which they live.
https://www.pexels.com/photo/different-artifacts-on-the-black-table-7189440/

Rromanipé or the Gypsy World View

Rromanipé encompasses the ideas of honor, dignity, and justice. As mentioned, the gypsies do not have a common religion; instead, they follow the faith of the host country. They described themselves as "numerous stars scattered in God's sight." The gypsies believe in karma, an element deeply rooted in Indian philosophy.

Loosely translated, karma can be defined as "spiritual balance" or "what goes around comes around." According to Romani philosophy, there is a constant conflict between the Devil and the divine in every human being. The one who wins this conflict decides how your life turns out.

Another important facet of Rromanipé is respect for elders. They strongly believe that when anyone disrespects elders, the ancestor spirits do not rest until the perpetrator is taught a lesson and disciplined. The Romani addressed their god through various names, including Devlam, Devla, Del, and more, and these words have been part of the Romani language since ancient times.

Devla means "God." For the Roma novice, it is important to distinguish this word from the English word "devil." In the Romani language, the word for devil is "beng." Devla is etymologically related to the Sanskrit word "Dev," which means god.

The Roma believe in a spiritual higher power or energy referred to as "dji." This spiritual energy gets diminished when they spend time outside their community, which is why they hesitate to assimilate with non-Roma people and are highly suspicious of outsiders.

In fact, having a distant gypsy cousin does not mean you will be accepted into the Romani fold. Further, one gypsy might not consider another as part of the family or kampania (or kumpania) if the rules and regulations are not strictly adhered to. The ones who do not follow the laws are ostracized and expelled from the community. The gypsies refer to non-gypsies as "Gorgers."

Another interesting aspect of Romano rules is that everything in this world is categorized as elements that are clean and or marime (dirty). Being or becoming marime or coming in contact with anything marime can cause a lot of pain and harm to the victim. You could get bad luck, become sick, contract a disease, and even die. Many things are considered marime, according to Rromanipé. Some of them are:

- Liquid coming out of our bodies (for example, urine)
- Rodents
- Reptiles
- Anything that touches the ground

Once an item is considered marime, the Romani people avoid all contact with it or at least limit contact with the element. The concept of marime and what elements are "dirty" are instilled into them right from birth. Avoiding "dirty" impacts how gypsies live, act, think, and speak.

Further, if a tangible object is considered marime, the words used to describe or name it are also marime. For example, menstruation is marime. Thus, periods and menses are not discussed, nor are the words used in conversation. The Romani language does not have a word for menstruation or many other marime conditions. They are simply referred to as "things." Sometimes, they are given descriptions such as long things, short things, difficult things, bad things, etc.

While certain conditions, such as menstruation, are marime, people experiencing marime conditions are also given special treatment because they can spread marime. For example, women during their menstruation are kept separate. The same holds for people who are ill. If someone is ill, their things are segregated from the rest of the stuff in the home because the illness—which is considered marime—can spread.

The good thing is that people affected by marime conditions are not spoken of in any negative connotation. This is because the Romani believe that marime can also spread through our thoughts. The power of the mind—especially bad or negative thoughts about the affected person—can attract illness or the marime from menstruating women.

Suppose someone is ill in the house. Not giving sympathy to that person or being spiteful can also bring sickness to you. The negative thoughts in your mind "capture" the illness in your body.

The ideas of the Roma people might seem unscientific and illogical to a novice. However, it is not that they do not know how diseases spread; they are more concerned about why certain conditions are caught by some and not by others. The concept of marime is so deeply ingrained in the Roma psyche that it is believed that you can catch not only diseases but also unfortunate events—such as accidents or broken bones—by associating yourself or thinking badly about the affected person, especially those who do not follow Rromano rules.

This is why outsiders—considered marime—are not easily allowed to be assimilated into the Roma fold. According to Rromano, the most marime people are those who do not follow the code of conduct, cleaning rules, and other Roma rituals, which translates to everything outside the kumpania.

Even washing the dishes is done ritualistically. The order of washing is dependent on the amount of contact the dish has had with the human body. The dishes that come directly in contact with the human body are washed first in the cleanest water. Therefore, cups that touch our lips are washed first—with the purest water—and plates and pots only touched by our hands are washed last. Food from pots is transferred to the plate before it is eaten. A Roma will never take food directly from the pot and put it into their mouth.

Most importantly, dishes must be washed using running water, not stagnant water. Considering all these restrictions and rules, living the life of a nomadic Roma can be quite challenging and stressful. They are always thinking of how to avoid marime and live life according to Rromano, lest they get punished.

Gypsy Lore

Baba Fingo — Legend has it that Baba Fingo was the leader of the Romani people in ancient Egypt. The Roma were persecuted, oppressed, and severely discriminated against by the Pharaoh of Egypt. Baba Fingo led his people to the Red Sea to escape the oppressive regime so that they could hide under the water and be safe from the atrocities of Egyptian soldiers.

The Roma community in Egypt believes that on May 6, every year, Baba Fingo is resurrected, and the day is celebrated as an annual festival called the Kakava Festival, specifically in the northwestern provinces of Turkey. This festival is also connected to the ancient tradition of Hıdırellez, a celebration of the coming of spring. The Roma believe that the Kakava Festival brings blessings and abundance to all the participants.

The Legend of Bibi — Bibijako Djive is one of the most important festivals celebrated by the Romani people following the Eastern Orthodox Christian belief. The faith in Bibi and her legendary powers are connected with the Roma community in Serbia. The celebration of this festival is to appease Bibi, the goddess of cholera, so the Roma children are not affected by the disease. Bibi's legend goes as follows.

According to a paper published by Svetlana M Cirkovic entitled "Bibi and Bibijako Djive in Serbia" in the *Academia Journal*, Kona was an Eastern Orthodox Christian Roma settled in Serbia. She died in 1935 at the age of 99. She is believed to have seen Bibi for the first time. This legend claims that one day on a cold winter evening, when Kona and her family were finishing supper, there was a knock at the door. Kona's husband opened the door to see Bibi standing outside. She was tall, skinny, and bony. She wore a red dress, had long dark hair, and was barefoot. With her were two girls dressed in white and two lambs.

The husband invited them in and told Bibi she seemed very tired and asked her to sit down and relax. He also asked her if she was hungry. Bibi asked the family for a pair of peasant shoes because she was barefoot. Kona found a pair and gave it to Bibi.

The instant Kona gave the pair of peasant shoes to Bibi, she, along with the children and the lambs, vanished into thin air. The main door remained shut, and Kona's family heard Bibi's voice saying, "May God always give you and your family everything you need."

The surprised couple opened the door and went outside, hoping to see Bibi. However, she was knocking on the neighbor's door, a wealthy Serbian household. The rich Serbian woman opened the door and chased Bibi away rudely. Bibi cursed the rich family and returned to Kona's home, where she decided to spend the night with her two children and the lambs.

After being fed and warmed, Bibi put her children to sleep and said to Kona, "I am Cholera, and I have suffocated the children of your rich but rude neighbor. Celebrate my feast every year and make an inscription (Zapis) for my children on that day. Shout out loud the following verse, 'To the health of the Aunt and her children.'"

The family then turned in for the night. When they woke up the next morning, Bibi and her children were not found anywhere. Suddenly, loud wails were heard from the neighbor's house. When Kona and her husband went to see what happened, they realized the children of the rich household were all dead. From that day onward, the Roma celebrate Bibi and her children.

In Serbia, the word for aunt is *Tetka*. When the Romani people adopted the divine Aunt into their worship, they christened her Bibi, which is Aunt in the Romani language. The Roma now believe that the children of those who do not celebrate Bibi on that day—as ordained by her—are cursed to die.

Gypsy lore is filled with miracles and dreams involving Bibi. The Romani people believe that if Bibi came in their dreams, she would usually ask for a certain task to be completed concerning her feast or the way she expected to be honored. Sometimes, she would appear in the dreams of those who did not celebrate her feast. The Romani people's faith in Bibi and her miraculous powers is legendary.

Dhampirs — Dhampirs are protectors and guardians, specifically for the protection of the Moroi, an ancient, magical race of benevolent vampires with fangs that feed on blood. The Moroi do not wear capes, sleep in coffins, or turn into bats. They don't like the daylight like the maleficent vampires. However, the Moroi are not eternal and do not need humans to survive.

Dhampirs are part-Moroi and part-human and are dedicated to protecting the Moroi from their monstrous, deadly counterparts, the Strigoi. Dhampirs are born with excellent reflexes, amazing agility, increased strength and power, and outstanding endurance.

Today, dhampirs are famous in entertainment as they are included in multiple fantasy films and books. However, the idea of dhampirs is rooted in gypsy folklore. It is the name given to the child of a vampire by the Slavonic gypsies. According to gypsy lore, the child has a few vampire powers. The story of how dhampirs are born is also found in gypsy lore.

It is believed that when a new vampire wakes up, he is extremely aroused. Since he is new and has not yet found a vampire mate, he goes in search of the widow he has left behind in the human world to satiate his sexual desires. If he does not have a widow for this purpose, he just finds any young woman.

The widow or the young woman can get impregnated by the new vampire, and the baby born out of this union is a dhampir. The gypsies had other names for this being. The female of this species was called Vampira, and the male was Vampir. While there were varying beliefs about the kind of powers this special child had, there was no doubt that a human with vampire blood got superpowers in some form. Some of them craved blood, while others did not need it. The Serbian gypsies believed that vampires were invisible to humans, but dhampirs could see them.

Ursitory — The Ursitory is known by many names, including Urmen, Ursoni, Ourmes, Oursitori, etc. They are a group of three female spirits (or fairies) of fate or destiny. According to Romani folklore, the three fate spirits appear three nights after the birth of a child to decide their fate. The benevolent or good fairy foresees happy, bright future events for the child. The sad, pessimistic spirit foresees the worst things happening in the child's future.

The third one, the most powerful fairy, is the impartial one dedicated to sensibility and reason. She settles the child's fate after taking input from the good and the bad fairies. Her decision on the child's fate is binding, and once the fate is sealed by the Urmen, no one and nothing can change it.

Vampire Pumpkins and Watermelons — This legend originated from the Romani people in the Balkans in southeast Europe. The Romani people believe that watermelons and pumpkins have special properties. These two vegetables can acquire vampire traits if left out the entire night under the full moon's effects. The first and most obvious sign of vampirism is a drop of blood that can be seen on the rind of these vegetables.

The Roma believe that only pumpkins—all kinds of pumpkins—and watermelons have the power to transform into vampires. While some believe the transformation happens during a full moon night, others believe the vegetables turn into vampires when they fight each other.

When the pumpkins and/or watermelons are kept together for more than ten days, they begin to come alive, stir themselves up, and make growling sounds. The vampire vegetables and normal ones look alike, and it is impossible to discern differences except for the drop of blood on the vampires.

The vampire vegetables are believed to roam around the villages and gypsy caravans at night. However, they are believed to be harmless to people. Thus, most gypsies are not scared of vampire pumpkins and watermelons.

The codes, beliefs, and magical creatures and beings discussed in this chapter—there are many, many more—are why gypsies are scared of the power of sinister magic. Their belief is genuine, and just because non-gypsies don't understand it doesn't give them a right to mock or disrespect gypsy lore, codes, and beliefs.

Chapter 3: Gypsy Omens and Customs

The Romani often look at the weather and the nature around them for omens that may predict what may happen in the near or far future. Let us look at some of these elements and omens and understand how gypsies read and interpret their meanings.

The Romani often look at the weather and the nature around them for omens that may predict what may happen in the near or far future.
https://www.pexels.com/photo/a-person-covering-the-lighted-candle-he-is-holding-5435272/

Weather and Sky Omens

Gypsies try to read and interpret the meanings of weather, climate, and the sky above. They try to understand why and how weather and climate change, why the colors of the sky change, how the rain falls, etc.

While the modern world has scientific explanations for many natural occurrences today, the belief system followed by the gypsies can also be connected with these scientific reasons in small but certain ways. When we find this connection, it is easy to understand the working of a gypsy magician's mind. So, let us get to these elements and their meanings.

Rain

Rain is perhaps one of the most relaxing events that bring peace and happiness to most of us. Sitting at the window and listening to raindrops patter on our roofs and trees is so calming.

According to gypsies, rain symbolizes good luck, clarity, and cleansing. This is true because when it rains, all the muck and dirt on the earth is taken away by the rainwater into streams, ponds, and rivers, allowing Mother Nature to work on them and convert them into fertile soil and fertilizers.

Therefore, rain cleanses the pollution and dirt physically. Rain stands for cathartic cleansing as well. It is seen as a redeeming event, allowing us to clear our minds of negative and bad thoughts and lighten the burden of our overburdened souls.

Rain is also a symbol of calmness and clarity. Even when it storms, it stands for this meaning. This is because when there is a storm, we are all forced to retreat indoors, and we get the time to relax and look inward, which helps us calm down. The sound of rain is often like a lyrical, rhythmic lullaby lulling us to restful sleep.

You can speak to any farmer, and their first love is almost always rain! When it rains, crops and plants flourish, creating more food, wood, and many other survival elements and natural beauty, greenery, and other harbingers of joy and happiness for human beings. More often than not, the coming of rain and monsoons heralds a cleansing period and oncoming good fortune.

Rain also symbolizes rebirth and growth. It keeps the cycle of life going while helping plant life flourish and grow. Water is the symbol of life, and rain represents this powerful symbol. Without rain or water, life would not exist on Earth! And this is why rains are seen as bountiful and beneficial in the Romani belief system. So, if it rains on your wedding day, your married life will be filled with good fortune, abundance, and happiness.

Mist

Mist is commonly believed to be a mediator between the known and the unknown. It is believed to connect reality with non-reality elements such as dreams, illusions, divination, apparitions, etc. The Roma believe that early morning mist signals a good day ahead. For winter, it means the coming of more cold weather and wind.

Other Weather-Related Omens

The following signs foretell rain:

- If the sky has the color of a mackerel.
- If the sky has a greenish tinge.
- If you see a haloed moon or froth along the edges of a body of water.
- If you see a meat-eating animal like a dog or cat consuming grass or a cat scratching itself against the legs of a table.
- If you see snails in the twilight or the sounds of crickets are louder than usual.
- When you see cattle or cows lying down early in the morning.
- When you see swallows flying low.
- When fowl and/or peacocks call or sing.
- When you see rooks circling in the sky.
- When robins perched in low branches sing.
- When you see seagulls on land.
- When a rooster alights on a gate and crows.
- When you see mist high on the hills.
- When chimney smoke falls instead of rising, a storm is expected.

Other signs:

- When snow lingers in a place, more snow will fall.
- When it rains heavily in September, there will be a drought.
- When your fireplace is burning well with many sparks, cold weather is coming.
- When you see numerous hawberries, the upcoming winter will be cold and bitter.
- When you rub a cat and see sparks on its fur, cold weather is coming.
- When a cricket chirps inside the house, a cold winter will follow.
- When a blown-out candle flame smolders for a long time, the oncoming winter will be bad.

Mild winters or good weather can be expected:

- When the ticking of watches is loud before the onset of winter.
- When spiders spin cobwebs on the grass.
- When there is little or no smoldering when a candle is blown out, fair weather can be expected.

For weather-related omens, Fridays and Mondays have some connection with gypsy lore. If there is a storm on Friday, there will also be a storm on Monday. Or if the sunset on Friday is splendorous, it will rain on Monday. A warm October means a cold February.

Animal Omens

Animals and plants are deeply connected to the Romani way of life. They read and interpret animal behavior and sounds in different ways.

Here are some interesting weather beliefs based on animal omens:

- If you see a cat washing its ears, good weather can be expected.
- An old, weak cat dancing around unusually could mean the onset of windy weather.
- If a dog howls without reason, it signals an impending death.
- The Romani people regard Foxes as lucky omens, and their behavior toward you could bring a little or lots of good luck. For example, a good opportunity might come your way if you

encounter a fox while traveling. If this fox gazes at you for a while, it is an extremely good omen.

- The sight of a mule shaking itself is a sign of good luck.
- The sight of a moth hovering near a flame signifies upcoming good news.
- Seeing a white horse early in the morning means good luck will be with you throughout the day.
- Two horses playing together means happiness and joy in the family. However, if two horses are fighting, squabbles and fights can be expected in the family.
- If you see a crow standing on the road, your journey will be happy and/or fruitful.
- If a gypsy sees a dead crow on the road, they will turn back.
- Rooks are seen as harbingers of bad luck. However, if you have a property with a well-established rookery, it is a good sign. If the rooks leave after you buy the property, it is considered a bad sign or an upcoming calamity. Imagine buying a property with a rookery in Ireland, and suppose the rooks leave the nests within the year; you have the right to take back your money and return the property to the owner.
- If you see two magpies together, it is a good sign. However, if you see only one, it signals that a theft is in the offing.
- Flying wrens and robins bring good luck, while dead ones herald bad luck.
- If you hear an owl or try to capture or kill one during the day, it is an ill-omen. If an owl hoots very close to dawn, it calls for a human's soul and signals death.
- Seagulls flying over a gypsy wagon are considered an ill-omen, which means the death of someone in the family.

Other Common Beliefs and Omens of the Romani People

According to the Romani people, money and itching have a connection. If your right palm itches, you will receive an income, or someone will give you money. If your left palm itches, there is an impending expenditure, or you will give away money. If you put your handbag on the floor, it is believed that you will lose money.

Another money omen is this: Gypsies do not count currency notes in fours because it brings bad luck; they only count in threes as this brings good fortune.

If your nose itches, there are several connotations. One is that someone could slap you. An itching nose when someone is talking could mean the talker is lying. Itching feet could indicate impending travel. Itching in the right eye is a sign of ill luck, whereas if your left eye itches, something good will happen.

Bad luck omens — It is common to forget something while leaving home. Most of us would go back and pick up what we forgot. For a Roma, though, this will never happen because going back home after leaving the house for some task brings bad luck. So, the best thing is to manage the day without the thing you forgot or postponing the task for another day.

Red and white flowers represent blood and the gut. Placing these two flowers brings bad luck. Cutting nails on a Sunday brings bad luck. Burning flour or bread is considered an ill omen.

Umbrella omen — Opening an umbrella inside the house is irrational for the Roma and a sign of bad luck. Therefore, a Roma will never open their umbrella inside the house.

Omens heralding family fights — Spilling salt on the dining table is a definite sign of an impending fight or argument in the family.

Hiccups and omens — If you are hiccupping without a break and reason, it could mean that someone is thinking of you. If you can guess the person thinking of you, the hiccupping will stop.

Black cat omen — If a black cat crosses your path, turn around and find another way to reach your destination because, according to the Romani people, a black cat is a sign of bad luck.

Sharing bottle omen — The Romani people believe that sharing a bottle with friends or family is not a great idea because of the following belief: If you share a bottle of water, juice, or alcohol, you must have the last sip; otherwise, the other person is likely to steal your loved one.

Glass pieces omen — If you are a Roma, breaking glass might not be a bad idea. In some Romani weddings, the bride and groom each throw a glass on the floor. The more the number of pieces the glasses break into, the happier their marriage will be.

Shoe omens — Placing a pair of shoes on the table will attract bad luck. A pregnant woman should never wear new shoes because it is believed that both she and her baby will be put in a coffin! Therefore, the Romani people make sure someone who is not pregnant wears the new shoes first, and then the pregnant lady can wear them.

Other beliefs:

- It is considered ill luck for a woman whose ears are not pierced to have a baby.
- A newborn baby's hair is not cut until their second birthday.
- If you see a shooting star, it is a sign of impending death.
- When a tree is about to die, it is believed to "scream in pain." These screams should not be heard; therefore, gypsies cover their ears with their hands.
- If you see a woman carrying a jug of water, it is good luck. However, if the jug is empty, it is bad luck.
- Slicing an apple in half without cutting the seed means that person's affairs and wishes of the heart will be fulfilled.
- When two people utter the same word or phrase simultaneously, they must link their fingers and make a wish. If they do this, their wishes will come true.

Interpretations of Dreams among Gypsies

Dreams have long been believed to be the voice of the divine trying to send us messages. Gypsies follow their dreams and try to interpret them in many ways.

Here are some pointers on their beliefs on dreams.

- If you dream of bulls, snakes, cats, or knives, it is a sign of bad luck.
- A mule or white horse in your dream means good luck. Dreams of horses mean you will get some news.
- If you see a fire in your dreams, there will be a summons for you.
- If you see a big house in your dream, you could be jailed or arrested.

- If you see people or dogs quarreling in your dream, friends are coming over.

- If you see fish swimming, there will be a scandal.

- Your dreams during the autumn season will come true. If you can recall your dream(s) in the morning, they, too, will come true.

Omens about Days of the Week

The seven days of the week have different meanings and significance to gypsies. Some activities are disallowed on certain days of the week, while some can be done only on certain days. Let us look at some of these omens in gypsy lore.

- Sowing flax and using scissors and needles are forbidden on Wednesdays and Fridays.

- No bargain or sale can be concluded on Fridays.

- Washing anything on Saturdays and spinning on Thursdays is considered bad luck.

The Romani people always offer flowers to people they meet on the road as they travel. This custom comes from their nomad legacy. As the Romani people traveled from place to place, they offered flowers to strangers they crossed paths with as a gesture of goodwill and a sign of peace. The gypsies strongly believed the Earth was round and that what goes around comes around. That the Earth was round was also the basis for another thought process: If they stay too long in one place, the Earth becomes heavy; if they stay in one place for a short length of time, the Earth becomes light. Thus, the balance of the Earth would be impacted negatively. This is why gypsies do not stay for very long in one place and prefer moving. Therefore, traveling is the way of life for gypsies.

Chapter 4: Signs and Symbols

Since ancient times, human beings have used symbols to communicate and convey messages, much before the advent of written scripts. In fact, the power of a single symbol often can beat the wordy descriptions in an entire book. Symbols and signs are visual shortcuts to the subconscious mind, bringing forgotten memories to the conscious mind.

For example, if you see the symbol of McDonald's, many ideas and thoughts automatically rise to the surface. You could decide you are hungry and want to eat a burger. You could recall something funny or embarrassing that happened to you when you were eating a burger. You could associate people in your life connected with the burger or food. You could remember happy or horrifying sights you saw while chomping on your burger. The thing here is that without a single word being spoken, the lone sign conjures images and memories in our minds. That is the power of a sign or symbol.

This chapter discusses some of the most important gypsy symbols used in witchcraft practices.

Amulets and Talismans

Many gypsies carry talismans and amulets as good luck and protection charms. According to Romani's belief, an amulet is an item found in nature that is naturally empowered with magic. An amulet can also be artificially empowered—through rituals—with magic.

Talismans are not found in nature. They are human-made and charged with magic by gypsy witches or sorcerers. Typically, a talisman would be a coin or parchment paper inscribed with powerful magical words and/or symbols.

Gypsies carry their talismans and amulets in a leather or cloth pouch called "parik-til" or "putsi," which is normally hung around their necks. To the novice, this little pouch might seem nothing more than a decorative item. However, it is important not to be fooled because this little "putsi" could be filled with magical items.

The important thing about charms, whether amulets or talismans, is to keep them close for the magic to be effective in your life. If you find one or someone gives you one, do not put it away and forget about it. You can keep it in your purse or pocket, or make a small piece of jewelry with it, like a necklace or bracelet, and wear it on your body. Even during rituals, gypsies ensure that they keep protective and good luck charms that are used to enhance the power of the rituals close by.

Horseshoe

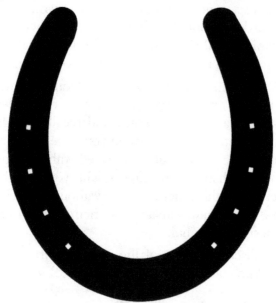

Horseshoe.
https://pixabay.com/es/vectors/herradura-silueta-suerte-negro-306844/

For gypsies, a horseshoe is a symbol of good luck and protection. All their horse-drawn wagons (*vardo*) will have a horseshoe tied to them for protection against evil spirits and for good luck. Gypsy women wear gold or silver horseshoe-shaped talismans around their necks for the same reason.

If gypsies find an abandoned horseshoe with its nails still intact, it will bring luck to the finder for an entire year. However, if it's found facing upwards, it signifies extremely bad luck. It's spat upon and thrown over the finder's left shoulder to prevent the ill luck from affecting the finder's life.

There is an interesting story about how gypsies came to believe that horseshoes bring good luck. Here is how the story goes. Once upon a time, there lived four demons: Death, Ill-Health, Bad Luck, and Unhappiness. One day, these four demons chased a gypsy on horseback. Bad Luck was swifter than the others, so he began to close the gap between himself and the hapless gypsy.

Suddenly, the gypsy's horse threw a shoe at Bad Luck, and he died instantly. The three brothers had to stop and bury their dead brother. The gypsy took the horseshoe home, and the three brothers plotted revenge against the gypsy. But the horseshoe continued to keep gypsies safe from the three vengeful brothers.

The Vardo is the most important possession of gypsies; therefore, a horseshoe is always hung over the door for protection. The vardos are all beautifully and colorfully hand-painted by the owners. The doorways are almost always exquisitely decorated, and the most gorgeous hand-painted horseshoes are hung over them. Horseshoes are used in weddings for the welfare and protection of the bride, groom, and their marriage.

Here's another legend from the Christian world explaining the good luck omen of horseshoes. There lived a farrier (someone who shoes horses) called Dunstan in the tenth century. One day, when he was shoeing a horse alone in his smithy, the Devil came along and wanted cloven hooves for himself. The Devil thought he would be able to travel far and wide comfortably as animals do with cloven hooves.

Dunstan agreed to the Devil's request but decided to help humanity with this act. Dunstan put the nails too close to where the hooves meet the skin, and the Devil cried out in agony. Then, Dunstan made a bargain with the Devil. Dunstan extracted a promise from the Devil that evil would not enter those homes with a horseshoe hanging outside the door. Only when the Devil made this promise did Dunstan remove the painful nails. Since then, people have used horseshoes to keep out ill luck.

Horse Brasses

Horse Brass.
https://commons.wikimedia.org/wiki/File:Horsebrass.jpg

The horse brass is an important gypsy talisman. Horse brasses are one or more symbols made from brass and hung from the horse's harness. Sometimes, many such horse brass plates are strung together on something called a martingale, which looks like a belt or strip of leather hanging from a gypsy's belt. These horse brasses were originally used to protect the animals from the evil eye and diseases and were also worn by people for strength, endurance, and fertility.

The symbols used for horse brasses include many elements from ancient times to modern-day belief systems, including stars, sun, moon, crosses, the three-legged sun wheel (or triskele), bells, images or plates cut in the shape of a horse, acorns, etc. Some designs have a heart at the base, symbolizing "giving heart" to the horse for increased strength.

The Hamsa and the Evil Eye

The Hamsa.
https://pixabay.com/es/illustrations/mano-de-f%c3%a1tima-hamsa-khamsa-3408067/

Evil Eye.
https://www.pexels.com/photo/a-blue-hanging-ornament-12133992/

The evil eye is a particular kind of magical curse believed to harm the targeted person(s) in the form of ill health, bad luck, and even death. Nearly all of us are targets of the evil eye or the dirty look, and most simply shrug it off as mere superstition. However, for the Romani people and many cultures around the globe, the evil eye concept is taken very seriously. Gypsies treat it as an extremely harmful malady that needs to be gotten ridden or taken care of immediately.

So, what is the evil eye? It is the evil look of someone intended to cause harm to the targeted person supernaturally. The evil eye can be in the form of a dirty look toward the target's good fortune, abundance, health, good looks, or anything that can invoke jealousy. It can also take the form of unguarded comments about the target and their good life. The health-related evil eye effects usually come in the form of fatigue, insomnia, diarrhea, and depression.

Gypsies, along with many other cultures worldwide, believe that diseases and sickness are rooted in medical issues and magic-related issues. A person can succumb to a malady not just because of a virus but also because of someone's evil eye attack. In fact, even objects can be attacked by an evil eye, which could result in the destruction or repair of the objects. This is the reason why evil eye protective talismans are hung over vardos.

The evil eye history is long and ancient. The gypsies have traveled all over the world, picked up all the elements across cultures and geographies, and used their lessons to protect themselves and their loved ones from the negative effects of the evil eye. The Hamsa is one such protective measure.

The Hamsa in the Hebrew language means "five." It's a beautiful, ubiquitous symbol holding different meanings for different cultures. It's often worn as jewelry. The Hamsa symbol is an upright palm with two thumbs facing opposite directions and three fingers between the two thumbs facing upward. The middle of the palm has a striking eye connected to the five fingers through different lines and twirls.

The Hamsa is known by different names, some of which are discussed below:

- **Hand of Miriam** — Miriam was the sister of Moses, one of the most prominent figures in Biblical history, the man who led his people out of Egyptian captivity and slavery.

- **Hand of Mother Mary** — The Christians call the Hamsa by this name, honoring the revered Mother of Jesus Christ.

- **Hand of Fatima** — The followers of Islam call the Hamsa by this name. Fatima, Prophet Mohammed's daughter, discovered her husband had taken another wife. She got this information while she was cooking. She became upset and dropped the stirrer into the cooking pot but continued to stir the steaming hot contents with her hand. Therefore, this hand became a symbol of fidelity.

When the Hamsa Hand faces downward, it signifies receiving, giving, and welcoming. In this position, the Hamsa represents abundance and good luck. It symbolizes welcoming good things into our lives, including good health, fortune and wealth, and happiness.

The Hamsa facing upward is a sign of protection. Wearing in this position protects the wearer from all kinds of harm and negativity. It also helps the wearer deal with negative emotions, such as worries, fears, insecurities, hatred, etc.

The eye in the middle of the Hamsa offers protection against the evil eye. Sometimes, the Hamsa hand has a lotus instead of the eye in the middle. The lotus stands for purity, regeneration, rebirth, and enlightenment. The fish on the three middle fingers are also for evil eye protection because fish living underwater are never directly visible to the naked eye and, therefore, free from the effects of the evil eye.

The Four-Leaf Clover

The Four-Leaf Clover.
https://pixabay.com/es/vectors/hoja-tr%c3%a9bol-de-cuatro-hojas-152047/

The four-leaf clover is considered an extremely lucky omen by the gypsies. A shamrock is a three-leaf clover often confused with a four-leaf clover. To put things in perspective, for every 10,000 shamrocks, there is one four-leaf clover—and the rarity is what makes it precious and lucky.

The four-leaf clover stands for love, luck, and hope. There is a common saying, "the luck of the Irish," and the reason for this is rooted in the four-leaf clover. Ireland is believed to have far more four-leaf clovers than any other place in the world.

The fourth leaf can be discerned easily because it is of a different green than the other three. If you find a four-leaf clover, it's a sign of good luck. However, if you give away this leaf to someone else, you could get luckier than if you had kept it for yourself. Multiple legends connect the four-leaf clover to good luck. Some of them are detailed below:

- The association of luck with the rare clover is believed to be directly connected with Eve, the first woman, according to Christianity. After being banished from the Garden of Eden, Eve is believed to have picked one four-leaf clover for herself before she left.

- According to Celtic beliefs, four-leaf clovers have magical powers of protection and can ward off bad luck and negative energies. The Celts also believed that if you carried a four-leaf clover, fairies—usually invisible and dangerous little creatures that can harm children—become visible, helping the wearer take protective measures.

- It's also believed that when Saint Patrick brought Christianity to ancient Ireland, he used the three-leaf clover to explain the concept of the Trinity: The Father, the Son, and the Holy Spirit. However, it's possible that Ireland—remember, it's the place where most four-leaf clovers are found—might already have associated magic and magical powers with this rare plant. The old and the new belief systems combined and enhanced the magical power of the four-leaf clover in Ireland.

One interesting final point about four-leaf clovers: If you find one, you are sure to find a few more in the same vicinity. So, do not stop with the luck of one four-leaf clover. Look around and multiply your luck by finding more.

Lucky Penny

Lucky Penny.
https://www.pexels.com/photo/silver-liberty-in-god-we-trust-1978-coin-64824/

The Romani people never leave a penny when they find one on the path they are traveling or anywhere else. The good fortune of a penny is not connected to its value but to the fact that it is made with metal, a scarce element, especially in ancient times compared to now.

Therefore, when someone found a penny, it was believed that it was a gift from God and that the finder would be protected against bad luck. The belief that metal is lucky is also one of the reasons why horseshoes are considered lucky. Finding a penny with its tail side up is considered bad luck in some cultures.

The Irish spit on a penny and throw it into the bushes so that they can be found by mischievous fairies and leprechauns and will give the person good luck. Another belief is that if you find a penny whose year stamp matches your birth year, your luck will be multiplied.

While you can buy good luck amulets and talismans from online and brick-and-mortar shops near you, it's even better if you can make them yourself. Use creativity to beautify your charms and wear them or carry them around to harness their power. Most importantly, when you make amulets and talismans, you transfer your powers and energies into them, customizing and personalizing them for your needs.

The next chapter teaches you the different kinds of amulets and talismans you can create at home.

Chapter 5: How to Make Amulets and Talismans

Just like wandering, nomadic gypsies, anyone who wishes to practice gypsy magic can learn how to create their own talismans and charms from scratch using easily accessible items they can find at home or in budget-friendly stores.

The word amulet comes from the Greek word "amuletum."
https://www.pexels.com/photo/glass-amulets-hanging-on-tree-6243236/

Differences between Amulets and Talismans

Before moving on to making amulets and talismans, let us learn how to distinguish between them. Both are magically charged with spiritual and/or magical power to protect against evil or bring good luck.

The word amulet comes from the Greek word "amuletum," while talisman comes from "telesma," which means "consecration ceremony."

Amulets have the power to ward off negative and evil energy. They either absorb or reflect negative energy targeted at the wearer. Horseshoes, coal, garlic, coins, crucifixes, etc., are some of the amulets people wear for this purpose. Amulets are magical objects that keep the person safe or bring good fortune to the wearer or holder.

Talismans, on the other hand, empower the wearer with positive energy so that negativity does not affect him or her. They are human-made objects charged with magical energy by gypsy magicians or talisman makers. Examples of famous talismans include Aladdin's magic lamp and King Arthur's Excalibur. Magic hats or rods carried by practicing magicians, etc., are also considered talismans.

These magical objects are worn or carried on the person to enhance the wearer or carrier's personal power. Therefore, talismans are amplifiers of a person's personal and magical powers. They guide the wearer to have the right thoughts. They need intense focus and should be crafted in specific periods and rituals.

Often, talismans are made of gemstones and crystals. They are usually a single piece, such as a pendant or a stone fixed on one's bracelet. Conversely, amulets can be simple bags filled with herbs, stones, and other magical objects. Amulets come in their natural form—though they could be magically and energetically empowered through rituals—while talismans are human-made objects.

Colors and Candles in Gypsy Magic

Different colors have different meanings and interpretations in gypsy magic. You can use this section on colors for all your rituals and gypsy magic practice, including making amulets and talismans. Candles are essential items in a gypsy's magical tool kit. They amplify and release the energy needed during and after rituals. You can use colored candles without lighting them for positive vibes and light them in rituals.

Black — Black stands for mystery and protection. It is the color of the clergy. Witches wear black to cloak themselves against evil and to protect their mysteries. It's used for psychic protection. Moreover, it's an all-purpose color—more so in black magic—and can be used for hexing, gathering information, learning new things, wisdom, shapeshifting, scrying, and more.

White — White stands for peace and serenity and promotes insight and personal strength. This is also an all-purpose color in white magic and can be used in rituals involving strength, peace, purity, unity, truth, young children, and balance.

Green — Green stands for growth and development and is great to use when you need your ideas to come alive. It is the color of life, prosperity, money, acceptance, weather, plant magic, and abundance.

Blue — Blue is great for emotional healing and for balancing the chakras. It is the color of communication, good fortune, willpower, concentration, organization, and sincerity, and it stands for the water element.

Yellow — Yellow is great for rituals involving building social and networking skills. It is also good for job opportunities and career growth. It's the color of happiness, success, memory, inspiration, magical practices relating to the Sun, and flexibility.

Red — Red is the color of love, sex, and passion. It stands for sexual potency, courage, danger, action, war, competition, and assertiveness.

Pink — Pink is for romance. Light a pink candle every day at your altar if you want to attract love. It is the color of compassion, femininity, maturity, domestic harmony, and spiritual and emotional healing.

Purple — Purple is the color for creativity and spiritual enlightenment. It works for rituals dealing with wisdom, spiritual power, independence, government-related works, and connecting with the spirits.

Orange — Orange boosts your ambitions and widens your horizons. It is the color of intellectual matters, self-expression, curing addictions, vitality, celebrations, and investments.

Brown — Brown is the color associated with all kinds of resources, especially materialistic resources. It is the color of pet/animal magic, earth, stability, finding lost things, real estate and construction, and food.

Essential Oils in Gypsy Magic

Essential oils are organic compounds extracted from plants and plant parts, such as bark, leaves, flowers, seeds, fruits, and roots. Essential oils have excellent healing and magical properties. They can heal the body, mind, and spirit and have been used for millennia to treat spiritual, mental, and physical illnesses.

Our olfactory system, which deals with our nose and smelling senses, connects these smells to the amygdala, the center of the brain that deals with emotions. It also connects to the limbic system that is responsible for our memories, stress-related issues, breathing, blood pressure, hormone balance, etc.

The above information is known to us through scientific studies in the modern world. However, the wise gypsies of yore already knew about this and used essential oils in their magical practices to harness their powers and magical energies. Here is a list of some essential oils commonly used in gypsy magical practices, such as rituals and making amulets and talismans.

Basil — Gives clarity and mental strength while stimulating the mind. As you breathe in the smell of basil essential oil, your powers of concentration get a big boost, too.

Bergamot — Uplifts you emotionally while soothing and calming your anxiety and feelings of depression. It is great to treat stress, grief, and fear.

Black pepper — Builds mental stamina and enhances the alertness of your mind.

Cinnamon — Great to use during times of worry and fatigue. Stimulates and energizes you.

Clove — Reduces mental exhaustion, anxiety, and depression and relieves stress. It is also known as a great aphrodisiac and is often used to treat insomnia.

Cypress — Aids in focus and concentration and relieves stress.

Eucalyptus — Soothes and calms the body, which is why people often use a few drops of eucalyptus oil in their baths. It stimulates the mind and helps to improve concentration.

Frankincense — Helps to slow down and deepen your breathing and is often used during meditation sessions. It grounds and calms you without any sedative effects.

Jasmine — Soothes the nerves, thereby building self-confidence and optimism. It is great for revitalizing and restoring energy levels. Jasmine is also often used as an aphrodisiac.

Lavender — Very well known for its sedative properties and soothes and calms the mind. It promotes sleep and reduces anxiety and worry.

Lemongrass — Refreshing and uplifting, it spreads happiness in the atmosphere. It combats nerve exhaustion and revitalizes the body and mind.

Myrrh — Helps mellow out heightened emotions and is a great meditation aid. It creates an uplifting and relaxing atmosphere.

Nutmeg — Removes doubt and resistance while improving spontaneity and flexibility.

Orange — Its sunny, positive vibes bring happiness and warmth. It helps to release negativity from your body and mind.

Patchouli — The smell is calming, grounding, and balancing. It gets rid of lethargy while sharpening your wit. It is great for meditation and prayer.

Rose — Aids self-care and self-nurturing by harmonizing the body, mind, and spirit. It helps you build self-esteem and aids in solving your emotional problems. Rose is also an aphrodisiac.

Sage — Commonly used for spiritual purification and cleansing. It helps us adapt to changes by bringing comfort and protection.

Sandalwood — The smell instills a deep sense of inner peace. It has been used in spiritual and magical practices since ancient times.

Vetiver — Helps eliminate anger, resentment, tension, and irritability. It also helps in grounding and is great for meditation sessions.

Ylang-ylang — Sedates the central nervous system, thereby reducing stress and anxiety. It helps us feel happy and grateful for life and what it offers.

How to Create a Simple Gypsy Good Luck Charm or Spell

As explained in the previous chapter, making amulets and talismans is better than purchasing them at a store. So, here is how you can create these easily using the methods given below.

Good Luck Charm with Paper

This is one of the simplest amulets that you can make for yourself. It is flexible enough to be used for any end purpose.

Materials Needed:

- Pens, different colored inks, and/or paint
- Paper
- Essential oils
- Candles

The use of essential oils is optional; however, they have magical perfumery powers that can enhance the amulet's energy. You already know how various symbols and signs are connected with good luck. Having these signs in your home or carrying them on your person will help draw cosmic energies to attract good luck into your life. Creating a good luck scroll with the above materials is one of the easiest ways to do this. Follow this process to make your good luck charm.

- First, cut a small rectangular piece of paper measuring about 4 inches by 3 inches.
- Mark the middle of the cut paper with the symbol of your choice using colored pens, inks, or paint. Remember to use pens with free-flowing inks, such as gel pens, fountain pens, etc.
- Next, write a small phrase or a few words describing your desire at the top or bottom of the paper. Then, add your full name, birth date, and other data that connect you to the paper.
- Now, roll up the scroll and use candle wax to seal it.
- You can anoint the scroll with your preferred choice of essential oil(s). For example, orange, nutmeg, violet, or rose are all excellent for good luck.
- Carry this scroll whenever you want to attract good luck.

What you write on the paper scroll becomes the power of the scroll. Examples of what your good luck scroll could contain include:

- I want a better-paying job.
- I want to attract love into my life.
- I want my ex to come back to me.

- I want to get into a particular university or course.

As you write on the scroll, repeat the intent as many times as you can so that the power is transferred to the scroll and it attracts cosmic energies aligned with this intent.

How to Make a Gypsy Mojo Bag

A gypsy mojo bag called parik-til was introduced in a previous chapter. You can make your parik-til for any intended purpose using a string pouch of any color of your choice, but use the color that is aligned with the purpose of the mojo bag. For example, if you want to attract wealth and money, use a green-colored string pouch. If you want to attract love, you can use a red one. The things you put into the mojo bag are entirely up to you. Here are some common elements that usually go into it.

- Oak leaves
- A stick of cinnamon
- Sunflower seeds and/or petals
- A horseshoe

You can add anything that you think will enhance the power and magic of your mojo bag. Put all the items into the drawstring pouch and dab or anoint it with your choice of essential oil, such as myrrh, cinnamon, benzoin, or prosperity oil.

"Parik-til translates to "holder of blessings." When you carry this bag, it means blessings follow you wherever you go. Therefore, hold the mojo bag you have created and feel the blessings emanating from it. Also, as you fill the drawstring bag with the items you have collected, you can chant a simple good luck mantra such as, "*I banish the bad clouds from my life, creating space for good luck. Come hither, come hither, good fortune, and fill my life with joy and happiness.*"

Gypsy Spell to Make Your Dreams Come True

- Sit down for this ritual on a full moon day.
- Light a white candle, ensuring that all artificial lights are switched off.
- Write your wish on a piece of paper.
- For about ten minutes, watch the candle flame and visualize the fulfillment of your dream. Then say loudly, "*As I lay down in*

bed tonight, may the cosmic energies combine to make my dream come true."

- Then, focus on your dream and burn the paper in the candle flame. Leave the candle to burn out completely.

- Repeat this ritual for twelve nights consecutively, starting from the full moon day.

Making amulets and talismans are all part of gypsy magic, and you can create your own depending on your need and the raw materials you have. You do not have to buy expensive stuff; t choose what appeals to your heart, use the right colors, candles, and essential oils, create a powerful intent, and transfer your personal power and dreams to the amulet/talisman you create. Wear it or carry it around so that the cosmic energies aligned with your intention find their way to you.

Chapter 6: Magical Herbs and Plants - A Little Herbal Grimoire

Gypsies have always relied on Mother Earth for their survival much more than normal settlers. Wherever they went, gypsies learned about and harnessed the power of common herbs and plants and used them in their magical and non-magical practices. Most gypsies have the skill and knowledge associated with using herbs and plants.

Gypsies learned about and harnessed the power of common herbs and plants.
https://www.pexels.com/photo/white-and-brown-ceramic-bowl-1793035/

If you want to learn the way of the Roma, mastering the knowledge of herbs and plants is vital. This chapter is dedicated to giving you a small grimoire of magical herbs and plants used by the Romani people.

Acacia — Acacia (also known as Arabic Gum) is used for spiritual and psychic enhancement and protection. It is great for rituals involving friendship, platonic love, and money. It's further used to aid in meditation.

Acorn — Acorn is a protective herb used in rituals related to personal power, wisdom, and good luck. Carry a dried acorn in your purse as an amulet to have youthful vigor and vim.

Alder — Alder trees are associated with divination and magic. They are also used in funeral rituals for the protection of spirits.

Ague — Ague is used in amulets for protection against evil and negative energies. It is used by itself or mixed with incense to break hexes and curses.

Almond — Almonds (also known as Shakad and Greek Nuts) are used to attract money, prosperity, and fruitfulness. It invokes the healing powers of gods and goddesses. It is also used for overcoming addictions and dependencies. You can carry an almond in your bag or use it as incense to attract the people you want in your life.

Amaranth — Amaranth is widely used in gypsy magic in various rituals, including healing broken hearts and summoning spirits.

Apple — Apples are used in rituals to honor deities. During Samhain ceremonies, apples are frequently used because they are considered to be the food of the dead. Apples are burned during this festival because they are believed to be the souls of the dead. Burning apples facilitate the rebirth of souls in spring. In the world of gypsy magic, apples are also known as Fruit of the Gods, Silver Branch, the Tree of Love, etc.

Balm of Gilead — This medicinal resin is mentioned in the Hebrew Bible and has deep connotations in Judaism and Christianity. It symbolizes love, protection, and healing and is used in rituals dealing with the loss of loved ones. Balm of Gilead is used in a love sachet to heal broken hearts and attract new love. It is also used to anoint candles. When it is burned, it attracts spirits.

Balsam Fir — This plant is great for building courage and strength. It brings about positive changes in your life, and if you are stuck with a puzzling question or problem, you can use balsam fir to find new perspectives and insights. Balsam fir is also used as incense by burning it on a plate of coal.

Bamboo — Bamboo is used for good fortune and protection against curses and hexes. Carve a wish or dream on a piece of bamboo, bury it, and watch this wish come true in your life. Another simple way to use bamboo is to carry a small piece on your person to attract good luck.

Barley — Barley is great for protection, healing, and love rituals. Simply scatter barley in your ritual space to keep out evil. Take a few barley grains and make a string with them. Tie this string around a little rock and throw it into a lake, pond, river, or stream while visualizing negativity leaving your body and mind and getting dissolved into nothingness in the water.

Basil — Basil is one of the most powerful herbs in gypsy magic and is used in spells and rituals involving love and wealth. The magic of basil also helps eliminate fears and evil and, therefore, is regularly used in exorcism rituals. If you know your path is filled with danger and need to move forward, carry some basil for divine help. You can carry a few basil leaves to attract wealth and prosperity or for success in a job interview.

Bay leaf — Bay leaf enhances your psychic powers. It is also used in good luck spells and rituals. As in the ritual using bamboo, carve your wish on a bay leaf. Hold it for a while as you visualize this wish coming true. Then burn the leaf, all the while imagining your wish coming true. Gypsies sleep with a bay leaf under their pillows to facilitate prophetic dreams. Carry a bay leaf in your pocket or purse for protection against black magic.

Beeswax — In the olden days, beeswax was the only raw material available for making candles. In gypsy magic practice, beeswax is used as a base for herbal healing salves.

Birch — The Romani people used birch for various magic rituals performed for protection, purification, to cure infertility, and exorcism. Plant a birch tree outside your home to keep it safe from evil and negativity.

Black cohosh — This plant attracts love, enhances potency (make a love sachet and carry it in your pocket for this), and increases courage. Carry it in a purple bag to protect against accidents and keep yourself safe from those who want to harm you. Add some to your amulet for courage and strength. Sprinkle it all over your house or room to keep out negativity and the effects of the evil eye. Burn it as a love incense.

Blessed thistle — Used to protect against negativity, blessed thistle is used by gypsies to break curses and hexes. Carrying this herb on your person will build your strength. It is also known to increase sexual potency in men.

Borage — The power of borage renders you with courage and sharpens your psychic powers. Put some borage flowers in your bathwater to lift your mood/spirit, increase courage, and protect your house from evil.

Buckthorn — This plant is used for good luck in court matters. Place buckthorn in your home to keep out evil and negative forces. Use the following simple ritual to make a wish or a dream come true with buckthorn:

- Make an infusion or powder of buckthorn.
- Hold it in your hand and face east.
- Turn in a clockwise direction standing in the same place until you return to your original position, facing east.
- As you make the circle, sprinkle the powder or infusion around yourself while visualizing your dream or wish.

Cactus — Cacti plants are great protective plants. They facilitate chastity and banish bad luck. Grow a few cacti plants in your garden to prevent unwanted energies from entering your home. Place cacti plants in all four directions of your home or garden for all-around protection.

Calendula flowers — These flowers are excellent for court and legal matters. Carry some in your pocket while going to court for the case to be decided in your favor. Putting some flowers under your bed will make your dreams come true. Another ability of these flowers is to render you the power to understand the communication of birds. Place some under your feet to understand bird talk.

Camphor — Camphor is associated with divination, psychic awareness, and dreams. Burn camphor to purify the surroundings. It also increases your power of persuasion. Add camphor to water when you are scrying.

Caraway — These seeds are great for rituals associated with love, passion, health, and memory. It has anti-theft properties as well. Place some caraway seeds in your safe or sprinkle some seeds around your house to keep out thieves. Caraway seeds are used in rituals and spells involving love and romance as they bring lovers closer to each other.

Gypsies use caraway seeds to consecrate their magical tools and knickknacks. You can carry it in a small sachet to improve memory. Place the bag under your pillow to recall your dreams.

Carnation — This flower is for healing, strength, protection, and balance. Burn it as incense to enhance your creativity.

Catnip — This plant is sacred to Bast, the ancient Egyptian cat deity. Catnip is regularly used in all rituals dealing with cats or cat deities. Catnip and rose petals in love sachets both give amazing results. Combined with Dragon's Tree, it aids in eliminating bad habits and behavioral problems. Growing catnip in your garden or near your home's entrance is great for attracting good luck and the blessings of benevolent spirits.

Cedar — Cedar is for power, confidence, money, purification, and healing. Cedar is used for consecrating wands. Make sachets to promote peace and calm. Hanging a branch of cedar in your home will give protection against lightning.

Celandine — Celandine is an excellent herb to cure depression and for assistance in legal matters. It brings joy and victory. Carry celandine with you to build self-confidence, especially when meeting adversaries. Celandine is a great aid when you are doing ritual work to release yourself or someone else from feelings of being trapped. However, please note that celandine is a poison and, therefore, should be used very, very cautiously. If you have even a grain of doubt, do NOT use celandine anywhere unless you are under the supervision of a trained and qualified person.

Chamomile — Chamomile is used to reduce stress, to heal, and in love matters. Burning chamomile as incense attracts wealth. Use chamomile in spells related to success and to break hexes and curses. If you want your gambling efforts to bear fruit, chamomile can be useful. Before picking cards in a game of poker, remember to wash your hands with chamomile infusion.

Chicory — Chicory's magical powers are excellent for promoting positive perspectives and enhancing your sense of humor. Anoint yourself with an infusion of chicory if you want to receive favors from others.

Cinnamon — Cinnamon is a spice that works excellently in rituals and spellwork involving healing, spirituality, love, power, luck, protection, passion, and wisdom. Burn cinnamon during meditation sessions to raise spiritual awareness, enhance your psychic powers, and attract money.

Cloves — Cloves are used in banishing rituals, achieving dreams, and protection. Burn cloves to eliminate gossip and its harmful effects on your life. It also cleanses the aura and enhances the spiritual vibrations of the area. String a few cloves together and hang them over baby cribs for protection. Carry it to attract love and help you during bereavement.

Daffodils — Daffodils stand for fertility, love, and good luck. Wear the flower near your heart to attract love into your life. Place fresh daffodils in any home where the inhabitants are trying to get pregnant. The flowers increase fertility.

Dandelion leaf — Bury some dandelion leaves in your garden or any other suitable place to keep your home safe from evil forces and negativity. They are great in spells involving making your wishes and dreams come true.

Dill — Dill is the herb for money, passion or lust, and protection. It is commonly used in house blessing rituals as it keeps out negativity. Dill also helps to discern mindless superstition and real magic. Dill seeds can be used in money spells to attract wealth. If you want a night of passion, smell dill seeds before bed. You can also add some dill seeds to your bath. Bathe in this water before a date, and you will be irresistible to your date.

Dragon's blood — Dragon's blood is burned as incense to enhance the potency of any spell or ritual because of its strong banishing power to eliminate negativity and evil. It is used in rituals dealing with eliminating bad habits and bad influences.

Elder — Elder is used in house and business blessing ceremonies. It is good for releasing enchantments and protection against negativity. It also helps the wearer deal with temptations to commit adultery. It's also used in funeral rites to help the departed soul's journey to the other world. A word of extreme caution about this: Elder roots, bark, and raw berries are poisonous, so they must be used with utmost care. If you are unsure, do not use it.

Elm — Elm is used by gypsy magic practitioners to connect with the world of the elves. If you want to stop someone from spreading bad rumors about you, you can use this simple spell: Write the person's name on an elm leaf and bury it in a safe place. The slander will stop. Elm is also used for protection against lightning and to attract love.

Eucalyptus — Eucalyptus attracts healing vibrations. To do this, sprinkle some dried eucalyptus around a lit blue candle. Eucalyptus oil is a great purifier, too. Eucalyptus leaves are a great addition to dream pillows and healing bags/sachets. Put a few leaves into your amulet to heal and reconcile differences in relationships.

Fenugreek — Fenugreek is used for rituals and spells to attract money and improve fertility. Put some fenugreek seeds around your home to attract wealth. Find a small jar and fill it with some fenugreek seeds. Add some fenugreek seeds every day into this jar. Money will never stop flowing into your home.

Feverfew — Feverfew is used for protection against colds, fevers, flu, and accidents. Keep some of these flowers in your luggage and car while traveling.

Flaxseed — Flaxseed is used in healing and money rituals. Flaxseeds keep out poverty from the home. Place a small bottle of flaxseeds for this purpose. Flaxseed enhances the accuracy of divination rituals and outcomes. Sprinkle an infusion of flaxseed in and around a divination ritual space before the start of the ritual.

Garlic — The magical power of garlic has long since been reputed to repulse vampires and is also used in exorcism rituals. It guards against negative and hostile magic. Hang some garlic pods in your home to keep the family united. When you wear garlic while traveling out, it keeps bad weather at bay. Gypsies used fresh garlic to heal the sick by rubbing fresh garlic over the sick person's body. The garlic absorbs the sickness from the individual, which can then be discarded safely.

Ginseng — Ginseng's magical uses include beauty, love, and healing. Carry some ginseng to attract love and increase libido. Carve your wish into ginseng root and throw it in water. Your wish will come true.

Holly — Plant holly in your home or garden for protective purposes. It is also used in love, marriage, and good luck magic. Males with low sexual libido are asked to carry holly plants in their pockets, which is believed to enhance their sexual prowess.

Hyacinth — Hyacinth, named after the Greek god of same-sex love and intimacy, is the flower for love and good luck. Hyacinth is the patron herb of homosexuals. Wear hyacinth flowers to protect yourself against nightmares. Its magical powers are also used to help with labor pains.

Hyssop — Hyssop is the most commonly used purification herb in gypsy magic. It promotes spiritual opening and enhances the power of vibrations. Therefore, it is the most sought-after herb to consecrate magical tools and items. Just sprinkling an infusion of hyssop on objects and people is great to cleanse and purify them. Hang some hyssop in your home to protect it from burglars and trespassers.

Irish moss — Irish moss is an amazing good luck herb. Place some Irish moss under your rug to attract wealth into your home. Carry some for protection when you travel. Irish moss is used to stuff sachets or poppets made for money or love. Sprinkle an infusion of Irish moss around your business place to get increased footfalls.

Jasmine — Jasmine is used in rituals involving snakebite antidotes and for divination work. Jasmine is commonly used to charge quartz crystals. Use jasmine flowers in sachets to attract your soulmate. Burning dried jasmine leaves before sleeping helps to induce prophetic dreams. It also improves creativity and promotes innovation.

Kava Kava — Kava Kava can form a potent sacramental drink and is made as a magical potion that can induce astral work and visions. Carry it with you when traveling for protection, promotions, and career success.

Lavender — The magical uses of lavender are in the realms of love, protection, peace, and healing. Lavender is known to alleviate symptoms of depression. Sprinkle some lavender oil in your bath and have a restful sleep. When combined with rosemary, it prevents lovers from straying. If you are anxious or worried, burn lavender flowers as incense to feel calm and peaceful. The ashes of the burned flowers can be sprinkled around your home to attract harmony and tranquility.

Lotus — Lotus is sacred to many cultures, including Egyptian, Indian, etc. Lotus flowers adorn many Indian and Egyptian gods. It is very useful for spiritual and psychic growth, love, and protection.

Myrrh — Myrrh is used for spiritual awakening or opening, healing, and meditation. Thanks to high vibrations of psychic powers, myrrh works well to enhance the power and energy of all magic rituals and workings. Myrrh smoke can be used to cleanse and bless talismans and amulets. Usually, myrrh and frankincense are burned together as incense.

Marigold — This flower attracts admiration and respect and works well in court and legal matters. Add an infusion of marigolds into your bathwater to attract love. This flower is excellent to use in love sachets and amulets to attract new love and intensify love and romance in an existing relationship.

Mugwort — Mugwort can be carried around to cure insanity and other mental illnesses. It is also good for lust and fertility. Placing mugwort near divination and scrying tools will enhance their powers. Rubbing an infusion of mugwort on objects is excellent for ridding negativity and cleansing the magical aura of crystal balls and magic mirrors.

Oak — Oak is believed to be the most sacred of all trees. Oak wood is used to build many magical tools. Burn oak leaves to purify the surroundings. This will help to strengthen family unity. It also reduces sibling and family rivalry. Carry some oak in your pocket to keep yourself young and healthy. It helps to gain strength and wisdom.

Passion Flower — As the name suggests, this flower is great for increasing libido and attracting friendship and prosperity. Place some passion flowers in your house to bring calm and reduce conflicts and arguments. You can use an infusion of passion flowers as a wash to reduce stress and arguments. Place some passion flowers under your pillow for better sleep. Add some infusion into your bath for five days to attract lovers.

Peppermint — Place peppermint in pillows to aid restful sleep and for prophetic dreams. Peppermint oil can be used to anoint household objects and home furnishings. It is burned as incense to enhance the vibrations of sacred spaces and for healing and protection.

Rosemary — Rosemary is worn to improve memory and, therefore, is excellent for students. It is also used to create dream pillows to prevent nightmares and is good for spells and rituals connected to health, love, and passion. Rosemary is burned as incense before rituals for purification and cleansing purposes. Before any ritual, for added protection, you should wash your hands with an infusion of rosemary.

Saffron — Saffron is a great aphrodisiac and is useful for dealing with love, happiness, strength, and healing. You can carry a small amount of saffron for increased psychic awareness. If you are sad or depressed, washing your hands with saffron-infused water will attract happiness.

Sage — Sage is one of the most common herbs used for purifying. It can also help in dealing with grief and loss. Sage promotes spiritual, mental, and physical health. Write your wish on a sage leaf and place it under your pillow. Do this for three nights for your dreams and wishes to come true. However, if you do not dream about your wish, remember to bury the sage to prevent any harm. Carry some sage for wisdom and improved clarity. Sage is used as an incense to clear and cleanse ritual spaces before the start of magic work.

Sandalwood — The Romani people sprinkle sandalwood powder around their wagons to keep out negativity. You can use a piece of sandalwood to heal broken wands. It facilitates concentration and, therefore, is good for meditation. Your wish can come true if you try the following wishing spell with sandalwood: Take a small piece of sandalwood and carve your wish on it. Then burn it, and visualize your wish coming true as it burns.

Tea leaves — Tea leaves used in amulets and talismans are great for building courage and strength. It is also known to increase libido, making it perfect for making drinks related to lust and passion. Burning tea leaves attracts wealth and money.

Vervain — Vervain is used for sleep, wealth and money, youth-related stuff, peace, purification, and protection. Keep some in your home for protection against storms and lightning. If you are having nightmares, place some vervain under your pillow. Put some vervain in your bathwater for mental and emotional cleansing, especially before practicing magic. You can put some in amulets for protection, especially for children.

Willow — The willow is believed to be a sacred wishing tree and is perfect for moon magic and divination work. It helps to attract and strengthen love and overcome sadness, grief, and depression. Wear a sprig of willow when you have to deal with the death or loss of a loved one.

Yucca — This plant is used in rituals and spell work involving purification, protection, and transmutation. Use yucca fibers to make a crucifix and hang it on your main door for protection against evil and negativity. Before doing a magical ritual, cleanse and purify your body with an infusion of yucca.

Finally, here is a very important word of caution. Do not consume any of the herbs, plants, and plant parts mentioned in this chapter without seeking medical advice. Burning incense also requires maximum supervision, caution, and care. Therefore, avoid it, especially in the beginner stage.

Chapter 7: Gypsy Tarot I. The Cards

Now that you have a good idea of the basics of gypsy magic, let us dive into the gypsy divinatory practices, starting with tarot. Reading tarot cards conjures images of old, shriveled, white-haired women wearing headscarves and looking into crystal balls. Yes, gypsy witches might have dressed like this, and, of course, there is an aura of mysticism around tarot cards. Yet, tarot readings give an insight into the various forces in your current state of life and guide you to make sensible, informed choices for yourself and your loved ones.

Tarot readings are great to give an insight into the various forces in play in your current state of life.

https://www.pexels.com/photo/assorted-tarot-cards-on-table-3088369/

Different Types of Tarot Card Decks

Over the years, multiple decks have been developed by different cultures around the world. Let us look at some of them in this section.

Rider-Waite Deck — The most popular deck available is the Rider-Waite Deck. It comprises the classic Major and Minor Arcana. It was first published by Arthur Edward Waite, a mystic and academic. The illustrations were done by Pamela Coleman Smith, and her name is now synonymous with tarot cards.

Thoth Tarot — This tarot deck was designed and outlined by the English magician and occultist Aleister Crowley and was first published in 1969. The illustrations were done by Lady Freida Harris, who created, modified, and recreated drawings according to Crowley's specifications.

The Wild Unknown — This deck is inspired and drawn from the ancient animal spirit and animal wisdom to interpret the present and portend future possibilities. It was illustrated and created by Kim Krans and first published in 2012.

The Enchanted Tarot — The Enchanted Tarot was created by the husband-wife team of Amy Zerner and Monte Farber. The cards were designed on the premise that whatever question a seeker has at a particular moment, the cards will reveal the answers and situations connected to that question. Tarot readings through this deck need not be done in person: Online readings are also possible because the intention is what matters.

The New Mythic Tarot — Illustrated by the internationally acclaimed Greek artist Giovanni Caselli, the New Mythic Tarot card deck features gods, goddesses, heroes, and demigods from Greek mythology.

As mentioned earlier, the first deck, the Rider-Waite deck, is the most popular, and most tarot readers use this.

Structure of the Deck

Here, let us briefly explore the structure of the deck, which is primarily categorized into the Major Arcana and the Minor Arcana.

The Major Arcana

The Major Arcana is the most easily recognizable set of cards in the tarot deck. The mystical messages they carry and express are both impactful and powerful. The twenty-two cards of the Major Arcana reflect different aspects of human life. The pictures and messages of the Major Arcana cards give you an amazing insight into your life path, dreams, purposes, obstacles preventing you from your purposes, destiny, and more.

Although each of the twenty-two cards in this subset of the tarot deck carries a specific message that guides you in your journey of life, collectively, they also tell you a story. The Fool, the first of the twenty-two cards, is the protagonist of this story. The Major Arcana is a journey of the Fool as he meets with each card.

As he moves through the remaining twenty-one cards, he grows and learns from life experiences. The story describes the various setbacks and accomplishments we face in our lifetime, all of which contribute to completing our fully-rounded personalities. Following is a brief description of the twenty-two Major Arcana cards:

Card #0 — The Fool — The first card in the Major Arcana, the Fool represents the most vulnerable aspects of ourselves. The Fool is inexperienced and unaware of his strengths, weaknesses, and potential. When you draw the Fool card, it usually calls for openness and willingness to embrace everything that will happen in the future and learn the lessons that the events and experiences are trying to teach you.

Card #1 — The Magician — The second Major Arcana card reminds you that you are unique and special. It tells you that you have it in you to do what it takes and get what you want. Your gifts and talents set you apart from the crowd. The Magician card tells you not to waste these skills and that you must harness them to begin new projects and/or overcome challenges and adversity. When you draw the Magician card, you should not wait any longer: You should move forward and accomplish your goals.

Card #2 — The High Priestess — This indicates our subconscious mind and awareness. It is the most intuitive card in the entire tarot card deck. It reminds you that your mind knows far more than you think. This card indicates that you should follow your heart and trust your instincts. If you draw the High Priestess card, it's a sign to stop looking outward and turn inward to find the answers you seek.

Card #3 — The Empress — The Empress, deeply connected to Mother Earth, manifests all things feminine, including beauty, love, and compassion. The Empress urges you to embrace everything the world offers you in any given situation so that you can harness all the energy to achieve your desired outcomes.

Card #4 — The Emperor — The Emperor stands for authority and power. This card is a sign of organizational power and leadership. This card reminds you that just like an emperor, you must also face and overcome challenges to become the king of your life. If you get this card, it is a message that you also hold great control over your life and how you want it to pan out.

Card #5 — The Hierophant — The Hierophant is a messenger from the heavens who carries the wisdom, spirituality, and knowledge he gained there to the human world. If you draw the Hierophant card, it indicates following the rules and regulations in that particular situation if you have to win. Moreover, it's also an indication to find a spiritual perspective of the circumstance under consideration.

Card #6 — The Lovers — The Lovers card does not just represent romantic relationships but all of life's close relationships. If you get this card, it means you need to focus on your love life. Normally, the Lovers card is drawn when you are at some crossroads in your life and is a reminder to recall your life's values and principles. The Lovers card urges you not to make hasty decisions and wrong choices. It tells you that it's your duty to look at all possible angles of a given problem and make informed, sensible choices.

Card #7 — The Chariot — Like a fast-moving chariot, this card is the manifestation of human determination and drive. If you pick the Chariot card, it could indicate an upcoming successful event or victorious endeavor. This card also reminds you that your greatest successes do not come from limited or narrow thinking. It tells you that if you combine the power of your mind, spirit, and heart, nothing can stop you.

Card #8 — Strength — As the name suggests, this card represents strength, though not necessarily physical strength. It is indicative of the power and strength of your heart and how courageous you are. It indicates your willpower and ability to deal with whatever life throws at you. If you pick this card during a tarot reading, it's a message that you have the strength to deal with whatever you are facing right now and will come out stronger and more powerful.

Card #9 — The Hermit — The Hermit loves solitude because he knows it is possible to find solutions and answers in deep silence. The Hermit card tells you that the best way to understand and process everything happening in your life is to withdraw from the chaos and noise. It tells you to find your place of solitude so that you can turn inward and discover the answers to your questions and solutions to your worries.

Card #10 – Wheel of Fortune – The Wheel of Fortune reminds you that life and circumstances are always changing like a rotating wheel. Sometimes, you find yourself at the top, and sometimes, at the bottom. This card tells you that nothing is permanent, and everything, good and bad, comes to an end. It is important to learn all the lessons that life experiences are trying to teach you.

Card #11 – Justice – The Justice card is a reminder that what goes around comes around. It tells you that every action and non-action has consequences. Your present life and what you are experiencing are the result of your past decisions and actions, and they are exactly what you deserve. If you draw this card, it is an indication that you need to examine everything in your life and ensure that you are as fair as you can be.

Card #12 – The Hanged Man – This card usually comes up when you are in limbo and unsure what to do in any given situation. If you draw this card, you are uncertain what to do or where to begin. In such cases, always begin with letting go. Letting go can be in the form of loosening your grip over something or letting go of the results and consequences of your actions. The Hanged Man reminds you that small sacrifices have to be made for the bigger picture to emerge in your favor.

Card #13 – Death – Sadly, this is one of the most misunderstood cards in the tarot deck. The Death card does not stand for physical death. It symbolizes cycles that have both beginnings and endings. While death does stand for endings, you must remind yourself that endings also mean the start of something new. Therefore, when you get the Death Card, it could mean that it is time to give up holding on to old relationships that do not serve your purpose anymore. It means it's time to let old, bitter, and unpleasant feelings and memories die so that your heart and mind are ready to accept new, beautiful things.

Card #14 – Temperance – As the name suggests, this card stands for patience and peace. If you draw this card, it is an indication for you to go with the flow, not to resist things and events happening in your life, and not to force anything to happen. The Temperance card is a clear sign that you must take things as they come to you, be flexible, and adapt sensibly to the changes in your life.

Card #15 — The Devil — If you draw this card, it could indicate that you feel powerless and constrained. If you pick this card, you will likely feel powerless and trapped in a situation you do not want to be in. The Devil is trying to convince you that you have no options. However, that is a lie. It is your life, and you can take back control of it. The feelings of being trapped have nothing to do with external forces. They come only with your internal limitations and the unwillingness to change, move forward, or see another perspective. The keys to unlocking your life are in your hands. You hold your freedom.

Card #16 — The Tower — The Tower represents destruction and is the most dreaded card in the tarot deck. It is normally drawn when all aspects of your life seem to be crumbling down, and there is nothing you can do about it. This card tells you to let things fall because the destruction also allows you to kill your weaknesses. Sometimes, you have to be an iconoclast to challenge and break down things completely so that you can use the remnants to build a better and stronger thing.

Card #17 — The Star — This card, representing healing and hope, calms and soothes. It brings renewal, optimism, and inspiration. This card means you are on the right side of the universe and that the cosmos is working for you. It is aligned with your needs and desires. Follow where your life is leading you.

Card #18 — The Moon — This card represents your subconscious mind and manifests your suppressed fears, doubts, feelings, and thoughts. If you pick the Moon card, it could mean that you are allowing your fears and doubts to overwhelm you and make you anxious. These fears might override your past happy memories and faith in a happy future. Draw these internalized feelings and thoughts to the surface, address them maturely and wisely, and worries and anxieties will disappear.

Card #19 — The Sun — This card of light and love represents optimism and happiness. If you pick this card, it means you are in a happy place in your life, and things are working in your favor. It means you are moving in the right direction. Listen to this uplifting card and identify and be grateful for the good things and people in your life.

Card #20 — Judgment — This card represents your past and future coming together. If you get this card, it is time to review what has been happening in your life, including your choices and actions, and see if everything is aligned with your ultimate life purpose and where you want to go. This card is a reminder that nothing is cast in stone, and you can change for the better at any time in your life.

Card #21 – The World – This card is a manifestation of a full circle of completing something fully and taking the fruits of your labor. This card means that you are exactly where you are supposed to be. It means that your self-awareness is high, and you have a much better understanding of yourself and the world around you than before. It means you are ready for the next phase of your life.

The Minor Arcana

The "minor" in Minor Arcana does not in any way take away the importance of these cards. In fact, of the 78 cards in a tarot deck, the majority belong to the Minor Arcana. The cards of the Minor Arcana provide you with insights into your life experiences in the short term. For example, it is useful to see how your day or week is going to be. It indicates what kind of struggles, obstacles, and successes you will likely face in the upcoming few days.

When you start with a tarot card reading every morning, the Minor Arcana card you draw will help you give your best to that particular day, no matter what bad and/or good experiences await you. The Minor Arcana in a tarot card deck is divided into four sets of fourteen cards each. The sets called "Suits" in the language of tarot cards comprise the Suit of Pentacles, the Suit of Swords, the Suit of Cups, and the Suit of Wands. Each of the four Suits is made up of the following:

- Numbered cards from one to ten. Number one is referred to as the Ace.

- Four court cards, including the King, Queen, Knight, and Page.

The Suit of Wands – The cards in this suit give you an indication of when to take action and when to lie low and hold back. It is the suit that deals with action and initiative.

The Cups – The Suit of Cups indicates elements concerning emotions, relationships, and intuition. The cards in the Suit of Cups give you the right direction in love matters and help you deal with all your emotions, from the smallest to the biggest.

The Swords – The Suit of Swords symbolizes challenges. They give you an indication of impending challenges and obstacles you are likely to face and how to harness your powers to overcome them.

The Pentacles — The Suit of Pentacles deals with finances, profession, and career. These cards answer questions related to your family, wealth, health, and long-term material goals.

So, each of these suits is an indicator of certain aspects of your life. The numbered and court cards show you exactly what energy patterns are affecting the aspects of your life. Let us look at the fourteen cards and see what they mean.

Aces (1) — Ones or aces usually mean the current period of the seeker (whether you or someone else) is at the start of a new adventure or venture. The card of Aces also indicates drive and determination.

Twos (2) — The card of Twos has two conflicting connotations. It means a dichotomous situation and also stands for balance. Therefore, you cannot move forward until the balance is achieved.

Threes (3) — Threes stand for interactions and communication and how your interactions with others affect all aspects of your life, including social, professional, and personal.

Fours (4) — A card of Fours stands for a break or rest. Rest and contemplation are essential for any journey to be successful. When you get a four card, it is time to take a step back and reconnoiter.

Fives (5) — Drawing a card of Fives means a time of conflict and adversity. This card tells you that it is time to draw up all of your energy reserves to deal with negative and unpleasant experiences. It could mean an upcoming loss, too.

Sixes (6) — Sixes stand for growth and development. It also means that you must find your inner resolve to beat the current obstacles and challenges to grow and develop.

Sevens (7) — This card is an indicator of your self-confidence. It tells you that regardless of the unpleasant things and events taking place in your life, you have the wherewithal to overcome everything, move forward, and achieve your dreams.

Eights (8) — This card tells you to prepare for changes. It tells you that change is constant, and only when you change and adapt will you find success and happiness. This card could be an indication that you need to reassess your current situation and change how you deal with it.

Nines (9) — This card is an indicator of all things, and your efforts are set to come together toward some sort of outcome(s). Of course, the result may not be something you expect or like.

Tens (10) — This card represents a finish line or the end of a cycle or period. It means you will receive the fruits and consequences of your efforts and actions.

Pages — When you get a Page card, you know what you want but are unsure how to get it. The Page card is a message that you must gather all the information and resources you need and then take the necessary steps to achieve your goals.

Knights — When you draw the Knights card, it is time to start work, take action, and set the wheels in motion. The Knight stands for movement, and you have to set about moving to get to where you want to go.

Queens — The Queen card represents your inner potential. However, it also means that you cannot do things alone. It tells you that it is time to seek the counsel of the wise and experienced people in your life.

Kings — This is a card of authority and power. It reminds you of your inner power and tells you to harness it to achieve your goals and desires.

Reading tarot cards involves many layers of understanding, including what you want to see and hear. Your instincts play a big part, too. The information in this chapter is a simple presentation of the various "tools" of interpretations.

It is entirely up to you, the reader, to come up with your own interpretations by tapping into your intuition and associating the meaning of the suite with the meaning of the card's number. The next chapter will delve deeper into this aspect.

Chapter 8: Gypsy Tarot II - Reading the Cards

In this chapter, you will learn how to read the cards like a gypsy. The Major and Minor Arcana cards hold life meanings and answers to our questions. When they are drawn and read together, they give credible messages that point in the direction of the answers we seek when consulting tarot cards. The ability to interpret the meanings of the cards drawn lies within each of our internal belief systems and narratives. So, let us get started.

1st Line

7	6	5	4	3	2	1

2nd Line

7	6	5	4	3	2	1

3rd Line

7	6	5	4	3	2	1

Start by looking at each of the cards and understanding what they mean. Focus on the illustration in detail. Next, focus on each card and think of its meaning both facing up and when reversed. Let's look at the 78 cards for this purpose.

Interpreting the Major Arcana

The Fool Card — When upright, it stands for innocence, a free spirit, and new beginnings. An upright Fool Card means you must get ready for a new adventure. When reversed, it stands for inconsideration, recklessness, and being taken advantage of or for granted.

The Magician Card — When upright, it symbolizes creation, desire, willpower, and manifestation. A reversed Magician Card stands for being out of touch, trickery, and illusion.

The High Priestess Card — When upright, it represents your inner voice, the subconscious mind, and your intuition. In the reverse position, the High Priestess Card represents repressed feelings, not being centered, and the disconnection from your inner voice.

The Empress Card — When upright, it symbolizes Mother Nature, fertility, and motherhood. In the reverse position, this card stands for a nosy attitude, smothering, dependence, and emptiness.

The Emperor Card — When upright, it represents fatherhood, structure, authority, and control. In the reverse position, it stands for coldness, tyranny, and rigidity.

The Hierophant Card — When upright, it stands for ethics, morals, tradition, and conformity. In the reverse position, it stands for new approaches, rebellion, and subversiveness.

The Lovers Card — When upright, it means duality, union, and partnerships. In the reverse position, it symbolizes disharmony, one-sidedness, and loss of balance.

The Chariot Card — When upright, it implies control, direction, and willpower. In the reverse position, it stands for aggression and a lack of control or direction.

The Strength Card — When upright, it is all about focus, bravery, compassion, and inner strength. In the reverse position, it is about insecurity, weakness, and self-doubt.

The Hermit Card — When upright, it is about inner guidance, the search for truth, and contemplation. In the reverse position, it is about losing your way, loneliness, and isolation.

The Wheel of Fortune Card — When upright, it stands for the inevitability of destiny, cycles, and changes. In the reverse position, it implies bad luck, clinging on to control, and losing control.

The Justice Card — When upright, it represents truth, clarity, and cause and effect (or consequences). In the reverse position, it stands for unfairness, dishonesty, and unaccountability.

The Hanged Man Card — When upright, it stands for martyrdom, sacrifice, and release. In the reverse position, it can be interpreted as fear, a needless sacrifice, or stalling.

The Death Card — When upright, it represents metamorphosis, change, the end of cycles, and new beginnings. In the reverse position, it stands for decay, stagnation, holding on, and fear of change.

The Temperance Card — When upright, it stands for the search to find true meaning, patience, and the middle, balanced path. In the reverse position, it stands for lack of balance, extremes, and excesses.

The Devil Card — When upright, it represents playfulness, materialism, and addiction. In the reverse position, it manifests restoring control, release, and freedom.

The Tower Card — When upright, it represents disaster, sudden upheaval, and broken pride. In the reverse position, it manifests fear of suffering, delayed disaster, or avoided disaster.

The Star Card — When upright, it stands for rejuvenation, hope, and faith. In the reverse position, it represents insecurity, faithlessness, and discouragement.

The Moon Card — When upright, it manifests intuition, illusions, and the unconscious mind. In the reverse position, it stands for misinterpretation, confusion, and fear.

The Sun Card — When upright, it means positivity, joy, success, and celebration. In the reverse position, it stands for sadness, depression, and negativity.

The Judgment Card — When upright, it stands for awakening, reckoning, and reflection. In the reverse position, it stands for self-loathing, low self-awareness, and self-doubt.

The World Card — When upright, it stands for completion, harmony, and fulfillment. In the reverse position, it symbolizes the lack of closure and restlessness about things not being completed.

Interpreting the Minor Arcana

The Suit of Wands

The wand symbolizes our innate power to draw the primal, cosmic energy that gets redirected in the form of passion, willpower, and inspiration inside us, all of which play an important role in leading happy, meaningful, purpose-filled lives. The Suit of Wands is representative of the fire element. Fire also stands for action and purpose. Therefore, the cards in this suit indicate your ambitions and subsequent plans of action.

Ace of Wands — When upright, it represents desire, inspiration, willpower, and creation. Reversed, it could mean boredom and a lack of energy and passion.

Two of Wands — When upright, it stands for leaving home, making decisions, and planning. Reversed, it means bad planning, fear of change, or playing safe.

Three of Wands — When upright, it represents rapid growth, looking ahead, and expansion. Reversed, it means frustration, obstacles, and delays.

Four of Wands — When upright, it represents celebration, community, and home. Reversed, it stands for conflicts at home, lack of support, and transience.

Five of Wands — When upright, it stands for rivalry, competition, and conflict. Reversed, it manifests respecting differences, conflict, and avoidance.

Six of Wands — When upright, it represents public reward, success, and victory. Reversed, it stands for punishment, lack of recognition, and excess pride.

Seven of Wands — When upright, it manifests control, defensiveness, and perseverance. Reversed, it manifests being overwhelmed, giving up, and destruction.

Eight of Wands — When upright, it means that you need to make some fast decisions or quick actions. Reversed, it stands for slowing down, waiting, and panicking.

Nine of Wands — When upright, it stands for grit and resilience. Reversed, it manifests doubtful motivations, fatigue, and exhaustion.

Ten of Wands — When upright, it stands for burden, responsibility, and accomplishment. Reversed, it stands for burnout, being overstressed, and the inability to delegate.

Page of Wands — When upright, it can be interpreted as freedom, excitement, and exploration. Reversed, it means conflict, lack of direction, and procrastination.

Knight of Wands — When upright, it stands for fearlessness, action, and adventure. Reversed, it manifests recklessness, impulsiveness, and anger.

Queen of Wands — When upright, it stands for joy, determination, and courage. Reversed, it means insecurities, jealousies, and selfishness.

King of Wands — When upright, it stands for overcoming challenges, leadership, and seeing the big picture. Reversed, it manifests unachievable goals and expectations, impulsiveness, and an overbearing attitude.

The Suit of Cups

The Suit of Cups is connected with creativity, intuition, and emotions and represents the water element. Cards from this suit speak about romantic, family, and platonic relationships and imagination. In a worst-case scenario, the Suit of Cups cards deal with uncontrollable feelings.

Ace of Cups — When upright, it means intuition, spirituality, and new beginnings. Reversed, it means emptiness, blockages in creativity, and emotional loss.

Two of Cups — When upright, it represents connection, unity, and partnerships. Reversed, it stands for tension, imbalance, and broken communication.

Three of Cups — When upright, it stands for happiness, community, and friendship. Reversed, it manifests isolation, gossip, and overindulgence.

Four of Cups — When upright, it stands for disconnectedness, apathy, and contemplation. Reversed, it stands for acceptance, sudden revelation or awareness, and choosing happiness.

Five of Cups — When upright, it can be interpreted as self-pity, grief, or loss. Reversed, it stands for finding peace, moving on, and acceptance.

Six of Cups — When upright, it stands for healing, happy memories, and familiarity. Reversed, it stands for independence, leaving home, and moving forward.

Seven of Cups — When upright, it means daydreaming, having to make choices, and searching for purpose. Reversed, it means confusion, diversion from your path, and lack of purpose.

Eight of Cups — When upright, it means leaving behind, walking away, and disillusionment. Reversed, it means fear of loss, avoidance, and fear of change.

Nine of Cups — When upright, it means luxury, emotional stability, and satisfaction. Reversed, it means dissatisfaction, smugness, and lack of inner joy.

Ten of Cups — When upright, it stands for dreams coming true, inner happiness, and fulfillment. Reversed, it means domestic disharmony, broken family, and shattered dreams.

Page of Cups — When upright, it means sensitivity, dreaming, and an upcoming happy surprise. Reversed, it means disappointment, insecurity, and emotional immaturity.

Knight of Cups — When upright, it means romance, idealism, and following the heart. Reversed, it means disappointment and moodiness.

Queen of Cups — When upright, it means comfort, calm, and compassion. Reversed, it means dependence, insecurity, and martyrdom.

King of Cups — When upright, it means to control, balance, and compassion. Reversed, it means bad advice, coldness, and moodiness.

The Suit of Swords

Associated with the air element, the Suit of Swords deals with intelligence, truth, logic, ambition, communication, and conflict. Interestingly, this suit is called "sword," and intellect and logic are elements that can be used for evil or good purposes, like double-edged swords. In a worst-case scenario, cards from the Suit of Swords can mean a lack of empathy, harshness, and abuse.

Ace of Swords — When upright, it stands for a sharp mind, clarity, and breakthrough. Reversed, it stands for chaos, brutality, and confusion.

Two of Swords — When upright, it stands for stalemate, indecision, and difficult choices. Reversed, it means confusion, having to choose the lesser of two evils, and having no choice.

Three of Swords — When upright, it stands for grief, suffering, and heartbreak. Reversed, it stands for moving on, forgiveness, and recovery.

Four of Swords — When upright, it means a time of contemplation, rest, and restoration. Reversed, it means stress, burnout, and restlessness.

Five of Swords — When upright, it stands for sneakiness, wanting to win at all costs, and unbridled ambition. Reversed, it stands for the desire to forgive and reconcile and lingering resentment.

Six of Swords — When upright, it stands for moving on, leaving something behind, and transitioning. Reversed, it stands for resisting transition, unresolved issues, and emotional baggage.

Seven of Swords — When upright, it stands for trickery, strategy, tactics, and deception. Reversed, it stands for rethinking an approach and coming clean.

Eight of Swords — When upright, it means self-victimization, imprisonment, and entrapment. Reversed, it stands for freedom, new perspective, and self-acceptance.

Nine of Swords — When upright, it stands for trauma, anxiety, and hopelessness. Reversed, it stands for hope and reaching out.

Ten of Swords — When upright, it stands for defeat, collapse, and failure. Reversed, it means the inevitable end, the worst part is done and dusted, and only upward movement now.

Page of Swords — When upright, it stands for mental energy, restlessness, and curiosity. Reversed, it means all talk and no action, manipulation, and deception.

Knight of Swords — When upright, it means defending your beliefs, action, and impulsiveness. Reversed, it means unpredictability, no regard for consequences, and lack of direction.

Queen of Swords — When upright, it stands for clear-mindedness, perceptiveness, and complex situations. Reversed, it means bitterness, cruelty, and cold-heartedness.

King of Swords — When upright, it means truth, discipline, and putting the head over the heart in all matters. Reversed, it means weakness, cruelty, and manipulation.

The Suit of Pentacles

Associated with the earth element, the Suit of Pentacles deals with all materialistic and worldly things, including finances and money, stability, security, health, nature, and prosperity. The cards from this suit also usually indicate matters relating to your household and career. A reversed card indicates greed, unbridled ambition, miserliness, and jealousy.

Ace of Pentacles — When upright, it represents new ventures, prosperity, and opportunity. Reversed, it stands for a bad investment and missed/lost opportunity.

Two of Pentacles — When upright, it stands for adapting to change, priorities, and balancing decisions. Reversed, it manifests being overwhelmed, losing balance, and being disorganized.

Three of Pentacles — When upright, it represents collaboration and teamwork. Reversed, it manifests group or team conflict, disorganization, and lack of teamwork.

Four of Pentacles — When upright, it means security, frugality, and conservation. Reversed, it stands for possessiveness, miserliness, and greed.

Five of Pentacles — When upright, it stands for insecurity, poverty, and need. Reversed, it means improvement, charity, and recovery.

Six of Pentacles — When upright, it manifests sharing, generosity, and charity. Reversed, it stands for domination and power, miserliness, and strings attached to help or support.

Seven of Pentacles — When upright, it stands for diligence, perseverance, and hard work. Reversed, it stands for not getting rewards or working without results and with distractions.

Eight of Pentacles — When upright, it means high standards, passion, and apprenticeship. Reversed, it means a lack of motivation, passion, or feeling or being uninspired.

Nine of Pentacles — When upright, it represents luxury, rewards, and fruits of labor. Reversed, it means false success, living beyond one's means, and excessive spending.

Ten of Pentacles — When upright, it means inheritance, legacy, and culmination. Reversed, it stands for lack of resources, instability, and fleeting success.

Page of Pentacles — When upright, it manifests diligence, desire, and ambition. Reversed, it stands for laziness, greed, and lack of commitment.

Knight of Pentacles — When upright, it stands for responsibility, hard work, and efficiency. Reversed, it stands for work without rewards, obsessiveness, and laziness.

Queen of Pentacles — When upright, it means financial comfort, creature comforts, and practicality. Reversed, it means smothering, self-centeredness, and jealousy.

King of Pentacles — When upright, it means security, prosperity, and abundance. Reversed, it means sensuality, greed, and indulgence.

Keep reading and learning about the messages and interpretations of each of the 78 cards in your tarot deck. The more you read, the more you will connect with the cards you draw, and the better your interpretations will be.

Shuffling the Deck

Before any reading, it is imperative that you shuffle the tarot card deck. This seemingly simple gesture of shuffling the cards holds a lot of purpose. It's a deliberate effort to connect to the deck's energies. Therefore, while shuffling the cards, feel them in your hands. Focus on the question you have. If you are seeking answers for another person, use the reflective time of shuffling to ask them questions in such a way that they will understand exactly what they want to know. Ask them to phrase their question correctly and accurately.

Do not rush through the process of shuffling. Take your time to ponder, think, and visualize the question or query. When you shuffle, you are effectively opening the portal that connects our world to the spiritual world. When completely satisfied with the shuffling, place the cards on your favorite cloth and begin the drawing process.

Reading and Interpreting Tarot Cards

Once you have understood the basics of tarot cards and what each of the 78 cards broadly represents, it is time to understand how to read them once you have drawn and laid out the spread—the classic gypsy layout is discussed in the next section. Do not just read out the cards and their meanings. Instead, create a narrative from the interpretations and meanings that each card gives you.

When you first start reading tarot cards, it is often done "by the book" and is a good method for beginners. As you start your journey, you will most likely be using your basic understanding of the meanings of each card to try and read a tarot spread. In fact, keep this book close by to look up the meanings if you are in doubt. You can also write the meanings on the cards themselves for ease of reading. Of course, if you don't want to sully your cards with any kind of writing or markings, keep this book handy.

However, as you read repeatedly and learn the meanings so well that they become part of your heart and soul, you must also harness the power of your instincts. Share your thoughts with the seeker as you pick up and read each card from the spread. Just remember to be kind and compassionate and not use words that suggest doom and gloom. The cards may give us bad news but also give us a way out of difficult paths. So, use that to convey messages wisely and maturely. And most importantly, everyone has it in them to change the path through the choices they make.

The Classic Gypsy Layout

Many kinds of tarot card layouts can be used for readings. We will be discussing the classic gypsy layout, which is a simple one but reveals a lot about the seeker's questions or queries. You can do this for yourself or someone else. It is a free-form spread, leaving plenty of room for flexible interpretations depending on the questions and your instincts.

After shuffling as described above, draw out twenty-one cards and place them in three rows of seven cards each, placing the first one to seven cards in the first row going from left to right, then using cards eight to fourteen to make the second row and again from left to right, and finally, cards fifteen to twenty-one in the third row from left to right. The first row is on top, the second row in the middle, and the final row at the bottom.

Reading the classic gypsy spread is quite easy and is done by looking at the past, present, and future. The top row represents the past, the middle represents the present, and the bottom represents the future. In the top row, cards one, two, and three represent the distant past, and cards five, six, and seven signify the recent past.

Look at the various cards in each of the rows, including the illustrations, derive the meanings of each card from the meanings given in the previous and this chapter—including reversed cards—dig deep into your instincts, compare notes with your questions, and lo and behold, answers will emerge very soon.

Also, you can read more deeply into this spread by reading the seven columns from left (starting from column one) to right (ending with column seven). Let us look at the columns in more detail.

Column one contains cards numbers one, eight, and fifteen and represents the self. These three cards indicate the most critical elements of the current question. Sometimes, the cards could mean the question that is being asked upfront. However, sometimes, these cards could indicate those hidden or obscure but highly relevant questions and related elements that need to be focused on for the current situation to be seen or experienced better.

Column two manifests the personal environment of the seeker, which could be you or someone else seeking answers from your tarot reading. This column consists of card numbers two, nine, and sixteen. The personal environment includes close relationships with family members, friends, partners, lovers, spouses, colleagues, and bosses. These cards show the seeker's relationships with these people in their life, or yours—if you are reading for yourself.

Column three, which consists of card numbers three, ten, and seventeen, represents the seeker's hopes and dreams. It is also the column that might reveal the fears and anxieties of the seeker.

Column four, made up of card numbers four, eleven, and eighteen, stands for the known factors and determinants in the seeker's current state of affairs. These elements could include the plans already in action, experiences that have already happened, or failures and successes that they are already aware of. It also points to what the seeker is currently worried or concerned about.

Column five, with card numbers five, twelve, and nineteen, indicates hidden destiny, especially surprises lying around the corner. When you read the cards in this column deeply, you will likely find impending unforeseen circumstances and hints regarding karmic justice.

Column six has card numbers six, thirteen, and twenty. It represents the short-term future and includes events and experiences likely to happen in the coming few months.

Column seven contains card numbers seven, fourteen, and twenty-one and represents long-term outcomes and resolutions. Sometimes, the ideas and meanings that have emerged from columns six and seven may converge and/or overlap. If there is a complete lack of overlap, it could indicate that an unexpected twist of fate is impending.

Ending the Tarot Reading Session

After the reading session, ask the seeker if their questions have been answered. If you are doing it for yourself, spend a few moments on whether you have got your answers.

If not, gently prod the seeker to ask questions they were previously uncomfortable asking now that you would have built a reasonably good rapport with them. If it is for yourself and you are dissatisfied with the reading, dig deeper into your mind and ask yourself if you are holding back something unpleasant or uncomfortable.

If the answer is still a no, do a reshuffle, and do not hesitate to repeat the reading. Take a short break if needed, and then do a second reading. You might wish to recharge your deck before doing the second reading. It's also good to wait a few weeks to do a second reading. Gypsies often wait for the current lunar cycle to complete before doing another reading for the same person with the same questions.

Whether the reading is done satisfactorily or unsatisfactorily, remember to give thanks to the universe for being with you during the reading.

Chapter 9: Other Types of Gypsy Divination

Tarot is not the only divination practice used by the Romani people. They use many other divination practices, including tea leaf readings, scrying—especially using a crystal ball— palmistry, and others. Let us see how some of these divination methods work.

Tarot is not the only divination practice used by the Romani people.
https://www.pexels.com/photo/gold-kettle-pouring-hot-water-on-cup-of-tea-230477/

Tea Leaf Readings

The practice of reading tea leaves left over in a cup of tea after the seeker has drunk the brew is called tasseography or tasseomancy. The tea leaf reader identifies symbols formed by the leftover tea leaves and interprets their messages. This is a simple but profound method of divination used by the Romany people.

The reason for it not being as popular as tarot card reading is perhaps because it is not very well understood—at least not yet. Let us rectify that mistake and learn some basics about tasseomancy. An 1881 text on tea leaf reading titled *Reading Tea Leaves* by an unknown author, who goes by the name "A Highland Seer," is the seminal document for most tea leaf readers.

Tea leaf reading is all about directing your inner energy to read and interpret patterns formed by the tea leaves left in your cup. Redirecting your intuitive energy is the foundation of all divination methods. When we focus on the leftover tea leaves, they become energy conduits and mirror our experiences, feelings, and thoughts, including the future. When we drink the brew with our mind focused on any question to which we seek answers, the leaves reveal relevant information. These leaves as energy conduits can also offer advice and foretell the future.

So, how does one go about reading tea leaves? The first thing to do is brew a good cup of tea—

although the process differs from brewing tea for usual drinking. You will need: A white teacup, hot water, and tea leaves.

You can use any tea of your choice and liking. Just remember to refrain from using tea from tea bags as their form does not allow for an easy read. Put some tea leaves into the cup. Next, pour hot water over the leaves. You do not have to wait for it to seep because the leaves will remain in the cup.

While you wait for the water to cool down, focus on your intention—if you are doing it for yourself—or talk to the seeker or querent about their requirement concerning the reading. This part of focusing on the intent is intended to transfer your energy into the highly absorbent tea leaves. Your question or intent must be specific because general queries will get you general answers that are often unsatisfactory.

When the water is sufficiently cooled, the querent—whether you or someone else—should start drinking the tea while continuing to focus on the intent. When about a tablespoon of the tea is left in the cup, the querent must swirl and twirl the cup. This is an essential ritual that has to be done with dedication and diligence. Ask the querent to hold the cup in their left hand and swirl it in a clockwise motion.

Next, slowly and carefully turn over the cup with the remaining tea onto a saucer and let it sit in this position for about a minute. Then, rotate the cup thrice and turn it upright, ensuring the handle faces south. If you look inside, you will notice that the tea leaves are arranged all around the cup in various clusters, shapes, and sizes, each of which holds insights into the intention/question.

There are more than 150 symbols that have been recorded in the book *Reading Tea Leaves*. You can use a resource that is freely available in the public domain. Let's look briefly at some symbols that the leftover tea leaves can form and what they mean.

The patterns formed in the teacup are generally categorized into five types: Objects, animals, numbers, creatures from myths, and letters with general interpretations.

Objects – A cross represents blockages. A heart could mean newfound love or improved harmony and love in an existing relationship. A candle or light bulb means new insights and ideas will come to the querent—or you, if you are seeking answers for yourself. Triangles are signs of good fortune. If you see a bed, the querent should take a break and get some rest. Apples are for knowledge.

The sun, as always, stands for happiness and success. If you see a horseshoe, you must make a wish. A sword, knife, or dagger could mean impending danger. If you see tea leaves forming lines, you are chained, or there is an upcoming journey for you. If you see plenty of dots formed by the tea leaves, increased activity is expected in the near future.

Animals – Fish are signs of good luck. Elephants stand for longevity and good health. Birds normally mean freedom, travel, news, or a message coming for you. A bee could indicate that the querent is going to be very busy. If you see a cat, it could be interpreted as some secrets coming to light. Butterflies represent fate. Dogs, as expected, stand for loyal friends. A lion means someone in a position of authority.

Numbers – Numbers usually refer to time. You must read numbers along with the patterns around them because the numbers could mean when something will come to fruition. It could be days, weeks, or months depending on what part of the cup the numbers are formed.

Mythical beings — A monster could mean a deviation from the normal. Seeing an angel could mean that someone is watching over the querent or they are protected.

Letters — Usually, letters represent the initials of people's names. These people are those connected with the query or querent in some way. You should look for forms around the letters that will indicate what role that person will have in the query.

Sometimes, you can easily discern the forms or patterns formed and what they mean. For example, you could clearly see the wings of a bird that could be interpreted as an upcoming successful journey or some kind of freedom. If you see a cross, it could mean blockages or obstacles in the path of the querent's intent.

Further, each part of the cup signifies a different aspect. The cup is divided into three sections for tea leaf reading purposes: The rim, sides, and bottom. The rim talks about the present, the bottom represents the far future, and the sides talk about the near future.

The cup's handle represents the querent's current situation and, therefore, should be placed facing south. The handle is the energy conduit connecting the physical and spiritual realms. Tea leaves near the handle represent events and people in the querent's immediate vicinity. The leaves on the opposite side of the handle stand for the querent's external influences.

Depending on the question, the sides on which the pattern of tea leaves are found can be used to determine the following:

- The timing — how sooner or later the expected event will happen.

- The connection — the distance between the querent and the person(s) involved in the event.

- Intensity — for example, leaves on the rim could mean a life-changing event is about to occur.

Scrying

Scrying is known by other names, including hydromancy, oculomancy, and crystal gazing. Scrying comes from an archaic English word, "descry," which translates to "reveal" or "show dimly." To the uninitiated, scrying is often connected with the image of a witch or gypsy, seeing the images of the future as she gazes into her crystal ball. We need to set this "popular but misleading" image right. Scrying is not about seeing the future because no one can really "see" the future. However, it is possible to speculate and predict what the future holds for querents using current information.

Scrying is an ancient art that allows you to see the future using the current data coupled with your inherent instincts and intuitive power, also called "second sight." Second sight, called variously intuition, instinct, etc., is an inherent human capacity to sense things beyond what our five physical senses show us.

The oldest available text that mentions scrying is a tenth-century Persian text called *Shahnameh*. However, every culture is known to use scrying in some form. A reflective surface such as a mirror, the surface of water, or a crystal ball is used for scrying. For example, the ancient Egyptians used oil for scrying. The Native Americans observe smoke to make predictions.

Here are a few common types of scrying surfaces:

- **Cloud** — Gypsies watch the clouds and the shapes they form to see and interpret the messages they are trying to send you.

- **Wax** — Wax is dripped onto a flat surface, and the shapes formed are observed and interpreted as cosmic messages.

- **Mirror** — Called catoptromancy, the mirror is the most common element used for scrying by modern-day gypsies. It involves gazing into a mirror until the scenes and images merge into one, and some pattern evolves.

- **Fire** — This involves gazing into the fiery flames. Even a flame from a candle or oil lamp will work (although observing the fiery flames from a campfire works best).

- **Eye** — In this rare but effective form of scrying, the gypsy practitioner gazes into the eyes of the seeker to observe the reflections in their eyes and discover and interpret meaningful patterns.

Here is a small write-up about how to practice water scrying.

Considering that water represents consciousness, it makes a lot of sense to use it for learning about and revealing to yourself the power, ability, and hidden aspects of your consciousness.

Materials Needed:

- A bowl made of natural elements such as wood, marble, etc. (brown or black is good).

- Water (preferably from a spring or river, or rainwater).

- Candles (two) with lighter or matches.

- Any small object (a quartz crystal will do fine).

- Energy cleansing materials such as incense.

Use a dark area to perform the scrying. If you are scrying outdoors, nighttime would be perfect. Make sure that you have sufficient space to place your bowl and candles.

Fill your bowl with water. You can collect rainwater if you do not have access to natural flowing water. Tap water or mineral water should be fine if this is also unavailable. Dark-colored bowls help you to focus better than light-colored ones.

Put the quartz crystal inside the water at the center of the bowl. You can use any object for this purpose. However, a quartz crystal is ideal because it has balancing, focusing, and amplifying properties that will help your scrying process. The crystal—or the object of your choice—will be your central point of focus. Use the incense to cleanse the aura of the place and the items of scrying.

When you are ready, light the two candles and place them on either side of your bowl in such a way that the reflection of the flame is visible in the water. Seat yourself comfortably in front of the bowl.

Enter a trance state using any method with which you are comfortable. For a beginner, chanting a mantra or playing a recorded tape of drumbeats should work fine. Close your eyes and focus on getting away from the physical world and entering your mind space.

When you feel relaxed, focused, and alert, you are in an altered state of mind. Now, open your eyes and stare into the water. Be patient because scrying can take time. More often than not, it takes multiple attempts at scrying to see what you want to see.

Now, focus on your intention and let your eyes dwell on the object. Gaze into it and allow the images that form to come and go. Don't try to hold onto any of the traveling shapes or figures. Just stay focused on the bowl and the object in it. Eventually, some clear pattern of words or forms will appear to give you the answer you seek.

Remember, the more you gaze and allow yourself to relax, the better you will access your unconscious mind, the space that holds many more answers than your conscious mind. Scrying is the art of trying to reach into your deep unconscious mind.

Palmistry

The uninitiated and the skeptics quickly brush off palmistry as mere guesswork, as they do all other forms of divination. However, there is a method to the madness of crisscrossing lines you see in your palms because they hold secrets that, if unveiled, will help you lead a more fulfilling and meaningful life. The art and science of palmistry are believed to have originated in India and involve interpreting the forms and lines on your palms. Here are some easy-to-understand foundational elements of palmistry.

The Shape of the Hand

In palmistry, there are primarily four kinds of hand shapes, each of which is associated with the four elements: Air, earth, fire, and water. While your hand might be the shape primarily aligned with one of the four elements, it is also possible for all elemental influences to be present in your palm. Here are the four types of hand shapes.

Air hands are taller than they are broad with upright fingers. People with air hands tend to be highly analytical and rational and put reason and logic above everything else. Often, they come across as being aloof because their minds continuously observe and analyze information and data from their surroundings. They might be sarcastic, but they respect fairness.

Earth hands are usually square in shape. They have fewer but deeper lines than the other three types. As with the reliable and practical earth element, people with this shape of hand are highly dependable individuals. They happily and efficiently take on the burdens of the world. They are not as bothered about emotions as they are about getting things done. They love to work.

Fire hands are normally found on people who ooze charisma and magnetism. Fire hands are often irregular and usually filled with lines. People with fire hands tend to be skewed toward fun and creativity rather than focusing on micromanagement or details.

Water hands are characterized by bony, long fingers and narrow palms, and the lines of a water hand are very fine. People with water hands are highly emotional, almost to the point of being impractical. Yet, they are very compassionate, highly receptive, and flexible to change.

The Three Primary Lines

When you think of palmistry, the three primary lines that come to mind are the heart, head, and life lines.

The Heart Line – The heart line does not answer questions such as the following:

- When will I find love?
- When will I have good sex?
- Who is my soulmate?
- Is my partner cheating on me?

In palmistry, the heart line represents your relationship or love style. The heart line manifests how you like others to relate to you and how you want to relate to others. The heart line tells you how you accept yourself. The heart line can appear in different ways on your palm, including:

It can start from the edge of your palm under the little finger and curve gently toward the index finger. The person with such a heart line usually tends to be empathetic, caring, and giving in a relationship.

It can start from the little finger as above and then dramatically move upward toward the middle finger. People with such a heart line tend to be highly passionate and deeply focused on their desires. They follow their desires passionately and also expect others to know their desires. They are very self-oriented people.

People with flat heart lines tend to have a romantic yet rational approach to relationships. They are thoughtful, considerate, and think very deeply about feelings and emotions. The minds of such people are on a continuous judging program, relentlessly thinking about feelings. People with flat heart lines also tend to appear aloof.

People with a short heart line—one that stops abruptly somewhere below the middle finger—are normally hermit-like. They love solitude to the point of appearing selfish when their sanctuary time comes. They love to work and are productive people. They just like to work alone and be alone.

The Life Line — Unfortunately, most people are under the misconception that the life line indicates the length of the person's life. However, according to palmistry, this is not true. It is the line that shows how anchored or grounded the person is. It speaks about your stability in life and your connections and relationships with loved ones and friends.

- A short life line indicates a hardworking person who constantly needs boosts of vital energy pumped, especially when the person is feeling depleted.
- A person with a thin, faint line could experience chaotic internal tension and feels scattered and lost.

The Head Line — The head line starts beneath the index finger and ends beyond the middle finger. This line reflects how your brain works and how we deal with data and information. There are different kinds of head lines in palmistry. Let us look at some of them.

- People with a flat, clear, and lengthy line are clear-thinking, love to integrate ideas, and love to calculate.
- People with a very long head line—one that is just a little short of touching the other palm—are those who are always collecting data and information, synthesizing and analyzing them. They have hyperactive minds that need to be engaged all the time.
- Those with a long head line but one that is frayed at the end are those whose thought processes never stop. Their thoughts are relentless and so fatiguing that, more often than not, such people find it difficult to reach any conclusion.
- People with a short head line are generally impulsive in their decision-making. They are more skewed toward their instincts and rarely overthink any matter.
- People whose head line crosses to the other side of the palm are usually those who can connect with people who have moved on to the other world. They usually have great psychic powers that help them communicate with gods and spirits. Such people also have problems dealing with the material world.

Mounts in Palmistry

Fleshy areas on the palm are called mounts and correspond to the seven planets in astrology, namely the Sun, Moon, Mercury, Venus, Mars,

Jupiter, and Saturn. Elevated and fleshy mounts reveal the person's balanced personality attributes. Sunken mounts reveal the person's weak or underdeveloped personality traits. Extremely prominent mounts reveal overemphasized and exaggerated personality traits. Let us look at the seven mounts.

Mount of Saturn — The Mount of Saturn is situated at the base of the middle finger and corresponds to fortitude, wisdom, and responsibility. It reveals the individual's integrity.

Mount of Jupiter — The Mount of Jupiter is located at the base of the index finger and stands for leadership, confidence, and ambition. It also reveals spiritual connections and divine attributes of a person.

Mount of Apollo (or Sun) — Situated at the base of the ring finger, this mount represents the person's dynamic essence, vitality, and optimism. This mount shows the person's potential for success, creativity, and happiness.

Mount of Venus — Located at the base of the thumb, this mount deals with sensuality, romance, love, and attraction. It reveals the person's indulgence, passion, and sexuality.

Mount of Luna (or Moon) — This mount is located at the base of the palm and beneath the little finger. It symbolizes intuition, imagination, and psychic powers. It reveals the person's ability for compassion and empathy.

Mars — In palmistry, Mars has a prominent role to play. There are three different sections on the palm representing three facets of Mars: Inner Mars, Outer Mars, and the Plain of Mars. Inner Mars is located above the thumb and represents aggression and physical strength. Outer Mars is located under the little finger between the Mounts of Apollo and Lunar. It represents perseverance and emotional courage. The Plain of Mars is located between the Inner and Outer Mars in the center of the palm and stands for the two Mars balanced.

The elements mentioned above are only the basics of palmistry. Once you have mastered the basics, you need to delve deeper and learn about other elements, including granular details such as finger position and shape, smaller lines branching off the primary lines, etc.

Gypsy divination is all about connecting with your inherent instincts to read and interpret the messages sent by the universe through various means. The more you practice these divination methods, the better you will get at gypsy magic.

Chapter 10: Gypsy Spells and Charms

In this final chapter, we will bring together all of the elements presented in former chapters, including herbs, symbols, omens, etc., and come up with various gypsy spells that you can try out.

The more you keep working with gypsy elements, the more magic you will attract into your life.
https://www.pexels.com/photo/tarot-cards-and-a-crystal-ball-on-the-table-7179792/

Healing Spell

Healing spells can be used for multiple purposes, including healing physical sickness and wounds, broken hearts, and even emotional pain. It is important to reiterate here that all healing spells should not be done in place of modern medicine but to enhance its healing power and give the affected person emotional and mental solace so that drugs prescribed by qualified medical practitioners work efficiently.

The healing spell described below is the simplest and almost free of cost. It's perfect for beginners who do not have the money or are still uncertain of the power of gypsy magic and do not want to spend money on spells. The key element in all spells—more so in this, considering that we are only going to use water for it—is your intention.

Make sure your intention is powerful and specific. Here are some examples:

- My migraine is gone. I am completely healthy.
- I no longer feel despair that my partner has left me. My broken heart is mended. I am ready for new love.
- My broken bone is healed. I can move my limbs freely now.

All you need is a glass of water. Use a clear glass for the energies to flow freely. Sit down in a quiet, undisturbed place and hold the glass of water in your hands. Say your intention out loud. Repeat it a couple of times.

Close your eyes, focus all your healing energies and visualize them being transferred into the glass of water. Once you feel satisfied that the water in the glass is filled with your positive, healing energy, it's ready for use. It has become enchanted with your energy. Drink this water and visualize healing energy entering your body.

Protection Spell

This protection spell keeps you—or someone else—safe from dangers. It is simple yet powerful. All you need is one white candle, a candle holder, and matches—or a lighter.

Place the candle on the holder and light the white candle. Next, close your eyes and say aloud the following incantation:

"May the light of this candle,

Protect me from all dangers,

Seen, unseen, felt, intangible, of this world, of the other worlds.

From all directions, above and below.

So, mote it be."

If you are doing it for someone else, use the name of the person instead of "me" in the second line. Say these lines a couple of times, and as you say them, visualize a white protective light bubble covering you—or the querent. Hold on to the visual for as long as you want. When you feel satisfied, open your eyes, thank the universe, and blow out the candle.

Good Luck Spell

We all love to have good luck on our side, especially during special occasions, such as a job interview, a promotion, getting admission into a good college, etc. Here is a spell that can attract good luck during such times. Again, the depth and power of your intention play a big role in the success of the good luck spell jar.

A good luck spell jar is great because you can carry it around—a perfect thing when you need it during an interview for a new job, promotion, college admission, or anything else.

Materials Needed:

- A small, clean glass jar with a lid or cork stopper
- Cleansing incense, you can use any one of basil, cinnamon, or violet
- 1 Green candle
- Chamomile
- Cinnamon
- Black salt
- Sage
- Cloves
- Rosemary
- 3 crystals: tiger's eye, green aventurine, and clear quartz

Light the incense and use it to cleanse all the items listed. As you cleanse each of the crystals and herbs, seek the plant or gemstone's help in getting you good luck for the specific purpose. Create an intention and repeat it as you cleanse the herbs and crystals.

Next, add each item to the jar while focusing on your desired outcome. You can hold each item in your hand and repeat the intention. As you hold the herb or crystal, visualize its good luck energy spreading its warmth into your system. Then put it inside the jar and close it with the lid.

Hold the jar in your hand and meditate for a while. Visualize your intended outcome. Next, light the green candle and melt a bit of wax. Use the melted wax to seal the good luck spell jar even more. As you do so, repeat the following incantation:

"I feel the winds turning today,

The wind of luck comes my way.

The skies are calm; there is no storm.

My dreams are true; they will be mine.

So mote it be."

This spell requires a lot of good luck ingredients. If possible, try and get all of the ones mentioned in the list. However, if you cannot obtain them all, try to get at least five of them to get an efficacious good luck spell jar.

Spell for Banishing Curses

The spell mentioned here is one of the simplest banishing spells available. If you feel that things are not going right in your life and believe that someone has put a curse on you and/or your loved ones, do this spell and let the curses out of your life.

Materials Needed:

- Cayenne pepper (a small amount)
- Sage (a little bit)

Take a very little of the cayenne pepper in your hand and add a bit of sage—the purifier. Mix the two ingredients in the palm of your hand using circular counterclockwise movements. Anticlockwise motion is for banishing, while clockwise is for attracting. While doing so, imagine the curse that you want to be banished being eliminated from your life.

When you are satisfied with the mixing of the two ingredients, go outside and blow the mixture out of your hand. Make sure you blow hard so that the mixture is completely and irretrievably scattered, just as the curses in your life. Brush off the specks from your hand and wash your hands clean.

Spell for Banishing Evil and Negative Energies

The spell detailed below is designed to keep evil and negativity away from your life. It is a bottle spell, so you can carry it with you everywhere you go, giving you an aura of protection. Bottle spells are brilliant for beginners because they are easy to make using simple ingredients.

Materials Needed:

- 1 small bottle with a cork stopper
- Rosemary (a handful)
- 7 needles
- 1 black candle

Cleanse and dry the bottle. Add the rosemary to it. Take one needle at a time and imagine all the negative elements and people in your life going into that needle. Imagine all the hatred and jealousy that you are getting and/or experiencing leaving your system and entering the second needle. Imagine all the evil in your body, mind, and soul leaving you and going into the third needle. Repeat the visualization until you have banished all the evil and negative spirits into the seven needles.

Next, place the needles carefully, one by one, into the bottle. As you add each needle, make a protection wish. For example, you can say, "*I am free of all jealousies and hatred.*" The rosemary—already in the bottle—will slowly and surely neutralize all the negativity transferred into the needles.

When you have added all the needles, close the bottle with the cork stopper and seal it. Here is what you need to do to seal it. Light the black candle and let it burn until you have sufficient wax to seal the bottle. Carry this bottle around and keep yourself protected from all kinds of negativity and evil.

Money Spell

Gypsy magic can positively impact your financial health and attract wealth into your life. The money bowl described below will help to increase abundance in your life. It is important, however, to remember that the money bowl is not overnight magic. Money will find its way into your life and stay with you over a period.

Most prosperity-related magic spells give optimum benefits when you align the magic work with the phases of the moon. Start with the beginning of the waxing phase.

Materials Needed:

- A clear glass bowl
- A few coins
- Cleansing incense
- A piece of paper and a pen
- 1 green candle
- 1 candle holder
- Essential oil connected with prosperity (jasmine oil works well)
- Ground or whole cinnamon, bay leaves, ground ginger
- Citrine crystal

Start by cleansing all the items on the list. Cleansing the items will remove all negative energies from the elements.

Then, write down your finance-related intention on the piece of paper. What is it that you want? A better-paying job? An improved bank balance? Make your financial aspiration as specific as possible. For example, you can write, "I have a job that pays me twice the salary of my previous job." If you notice, the example is written in the present tense. That is how your intention should be written—as if you have already got what you want.

You can write as many intentions as you want. However, if it is your first money bowl, make it simple and have only one intention. You can increase the number of subsequent money bowls you create.

Fold the piece of paper on which you have written your intention and put it in the middle of the bowl.

Enhance the power of your wealth bowl by anointing the candle with the jasmine oil before putting it on the holder and placing it over the piece of paper with your intent. Light the candle.

Next, put all the herbs mentioned above in the list of ingredients into the bowl.

Visualize your intention as you create the money bowl.

Ideally, the money bowl should be placed near your front door. Let the candle burn for about ten minutes. If it is not practical to do this, you can place it anywhere safe. After ten minutes, you can put the money bowl in your workroom.

Once or twice a week, when you feel drawn to it, you can add to your money bowl with any of the materials listed above. You can keep feeding your money bowl as long as you want. Ensure your candle and bowl sizes are large enough to last that long. If not, you can create new money bowls.

The spells, charms, and incantations mentioned in this chapter are only simple pointers to using gypsy magic to bring joy and eliminate sadness from your life. Learn and master these quickly. And then, use your imagination and the large amount of information given in this book and make your own spells and charms according to your needs and requirements. The more you keep working with gypsy elements, the more magic you will attract into your life.

Conclusion

Now that you have read the book, you must go back and read it again to put things in perspective. Read each chapter in detail, try and understand what is being said, and what lessons you can learn from it. For example, the stories of persecution explained in the first chapter teach you lessons of resilience, growth, and development.

The Roma did not take things lying down. They fought back, and even when they lost against cruel unfairness and injustice, they did not lie down for long. Like a phoenix, they rose from the dust and started their lives anew, learning and incorporating the lessons they learned into their new lives, yet not giving up the cultures of their ancestors.

Reread every chapter this way, and make notes about the various magical elements mentioned. The last chapter teaches spells and charms using all the elements learned in the previous chapters. Try all the spells detailed in the last chapter, one at a time, slowly but surely. Master them, and soon, the elements discussed in this book will be deeply ingrained in your psyche.

When you have mastered the beginner's lessons, move on and dig deeper into the world of gypsy magic. The deeper you fall into this world, the more you will discover yourself. Keep an open heart and mind, and find a new purpose in your life. Live life happily and meaningfully.

Here's another book by Mari Silva that you might like

Your Free Gift
(only available for a limited time)

Thanks for getting this book! If you want to learn more about various spirituality topics, then join Mari Silva's community and get a free guided meditation MP3 for awakening your third eye. This guided meditation mp3 is designed to open and strengthen ones third eye so you can experience a higher state of consciousness. Simply visit the link below the image to get started.

https://spiritualityspot.com/meditation

Bibliography

AA. "Roma Culture Comes Alive With Celebration of Baba Fingo." Daily Sabah

Alethia. "Scrying: How to Practice the Ancient Art of Second Sight (With Pictures). LonerWolf. Last modified August 19, 2021. https://www.lonerwolf.com/scrying/

A Little Spark of Joy. "The Ultimate White Magic Spells List for Beginners." Last modified January 23, 2023. https://www.alittlesparkofjoy.com/magic-spells-list/

Annie. "Gypsy magic: Romani Spells, Charms, and Folklore." Panda Gossips. Last modified July 24, 2018. https://www.pandagossips.com/posts/2055

BBC News. "On the road: Centuries of Roma history." Last modified July 8, 2009. http://news.bbc.co.uk/2/hi/europe/8136812.stm

Boswell, Lisa. "Real Romany Gypsy Life, Beliefs and Customs." #FolkloreThursday. Last modified July 12, 2018. https://www.folklorethursday.com/folklife/real-gypsy-life-belief-and-customs/

Bradford, Alina. "Roma Culture: Customs, Traditions & Beliefs." Live Science. Last modified November 27, 2018. https://www.livescience.com/64171-roma-culture.html

Chris. "Rain Symbolism (7 Meanings in Literature and Spirituality)." Symbolism & Metaphor. Last modified January 16, 2021. https://www.symbolismandmetaphor.com/rain-symbolism-meaning/

Cirkovic, Svetlana. M. "Bibi and Bibijako Djive in Serbia." Academia. Accessed December 1, 2022. https://www.academia.edu/42176038/Bibi_and_Bibijako_Djive_in_Serbia

Coman, Roxana. "20 Superstitions Only Romanians will Understand." Culture Trip. Last modified December 8, 2017. https://www.theculturetrip.com/europe/romania/articles/20-superstitions-only-romanians-will-understand/

The Cut. "How to Read Palms: A Beginner's Guide." Last modified September 8, 2020. https://www.thecut.com/article/how-to-read-palms.html

Faena. "5 Ancient Methods of Divination." Accessed December 1, 2022. https://www.faena.com/aleph/5-ancient-methods-of-divination

First Steps New Forest. "Superstitions." Accessed December 1, 2022. http://newforestromanygypsytraveller.co.uk/superstitions.php#:~:text=You%20mustn't%20cut%20a,can%20only%20bring%20bad%20luck.

Good Luck Horseshoes. "Romany Gypsies and their Lucky Horseshoes." Last modified June 21, 2022. https://www.goodluckhorseshoes.com/romany-gypsies-and-their-lucky-horseshoes/

Grauschopf, Sandra. "7 Lucky Superstitions (and Their Weird Origins)." LiveAbout. Last modified November 29, 2022. https://www.liveabout.com/lucky-superstitions-origin-895272

The Gypsy Haven Online Store, "Herbal Grimoire." Accessed December 1, 2022. https://www.thegypsyhaven.com/pages/herbal-grimoire

GYPSYWOMBMAN. "Colors & Meanings." Accessed December 1, 2022. https://www.gypsywombman.com/pages/colors-meanings

Howcast. "How to Cast a Banishing Spell | Wicca." YouTube video, 3:56. November 10, 2013. https://www.youtube.com/watch?v=OLkdl1k7dD8

Joshua Project. "Romanichal Romani in South Africa." Accessed December 1, 2022. https://www.joshuaproject.net/people_groups/11141/SF

Kelly, Aliza. "A Beginners Guide to Reading Palms." Allure. Last modified December 2, 2021. https://www.allure.com/story/palm-reading-guide-hand-lines

Kelly, Aliza. "Your Essential Guide to Tasseography, the Practice of Reading Tea Leaves." Allure. Last modified May 7, 2018. https://www.allure.com/story/how-to-read-tea-leaves-tasseography

Labyrinthos "Tarot Card Meanings List." Accessed December 1, 2022. https://www.labyrinthos.co/blogs/tarot-card-meanings-list

Lallanilla, Marc. "5 intriguing facts about the Roma." Live Science. Last modified August 28, 2020. https://www.livescience.com/40652-facts-about-roma-romani-gypsies.html

Lam, Hiuyan. "Hamsa Hand Meaning: Discover How to Wear the Hand of God." ThePeachBox. Last modified December 23, 2022. https://www.thepeachbox.com/blogs/jewelry/hamsa-hand-meaning

Leland, Charles Godfrey. *Gypsy Sorcery and Fortune Telling.* London: T. Fisher Unwin, 1891.

Parrs, Alexandra. "Egypt's Invisible Gypsies." Global Dialogue.

Petulengro, Paul. "Gypsy Traditions Today." Last modified November 19, 2016. https://www.petulengro.com/gypsy-traditions-today/

Romaniherstory. "The Ursitory." Accessed December 1, 2022. https://www.romaniherstory.com/fictionalcharacters

Shirleytwofeathers. "The Evil Eye." Hamsa – Sigils Symbols and Signs. Last modified September 24, 2017. https://www.shirleytwofeathers.com/The_Blog/sigils-symbols-signs/tag/hamsa/

Shirleytwofeathers.com. "Magick and Mystery." Accessed December 1, 2022. https://www.shirleytwofeathers.com/Magick.html

Tarot.com. "Tarot Card Meanings." Accessed December 1, 2022. https://www.tarot.com/tarot/cards/

Two Wander. "Tasseography: Tea Leaf Reading Symbols and Meanings." Accessed December 1, 2022. www.twowander.com/blog/tasseography-tea-leaf-reading-symbols-and-meanings

United States Holocaust Memorial Museum, Washington, DC. "Roma (Gypsies) in Prewar Europe." Holocaust Encyclopedia. Last modified March 19, 2021. https://encyclopedia.ushmm.org/content/en/article/roma-gypsies-in-prewar-europe

Wanderlust. "Determine Your Deck—the Many Types of Tarot." Last modified July 8, 2018. https://www.wanderlust.com/journal/determine-deck-many-types-tarot/

Watkins, James A. "History of the Gypsies." Owlcation. Last modified September 26, 2022. https://owlcation.com/humanities/The-Gypsies

Wigington, P. "The Romany Spread Tarot Card Layout." Learn Religions. Last modified March 11, 2019. https://www.learnreligions.com/romany-spread-tarot-cards-4588969

Wright, Mackenzie. "How to Make a Good Luck Charm Out of Paper." eHow. Last modified April 9, 2009. https://www.ehow.com/how_4897274_make-luck-charm-out-paper.html